TEACHER'S PET PUBLICATIONS

LITPLAN TEACHER PACK
CT Edition
for
Dear Mr. Henshaw

based on the book
by Beverly Cleary

Written by
Mary B. Collins
Dorothy Shelton

© 2014 Teacher's Pet Publications
All Rights Reserved

ISBN
978-1-60249-715-3

READ THIS
COPYRIGHT INFORMATION

This is copyrighted material.
It may not be copied or distributed in any way
without written permission from the copyright holder.

The purchaser may copy the student materials
for his or her classroom use only.

No other portion may be copied or distributed in any way.
No portion may be posted on the Internet
without written permission.

Copyright violations are prosecuted to the fullest extent of the law
and are subject to a minimum of a $500.00 fine,
imposed by Teacher's Pet Publications,
in addition to any other legal judgments obtained.

Copyright questions?
Contact Teacher's Pet Publications
www.tpet.com
or Mary B. Collins
mcollins@tpet.com

ISBN 978-1-60249-715-3

Copyright 2014 Mary B. Collins

Teacher's Pet Publications

Folks seem to really like the LitPlan Teacher Pack format, but the two most common requests we have had over the years are for more in-depth questions and more meat in the daily lessons. Now CCSS correlations are also a big request. So here is the new edition of the LitPlan Teacher Packs: LitPlans CT (Critical Thinking).

I've tried to keep a similar format while addressing the evolving needs of classroom teachers. Remember when I first created the LitPlans back in 1989, there weren't many other literature guides on the market, there was no Internet, and standards were mostly up to each school. Things have really changed!

The **Overview** section is intended to be a quick-reference tool where you can get a fast look at what is going on in each lesson—sort-of like the old Unit Outline, but in a bit more detail. The Overview also has grade-specific CCSS correlations for each lesson.

The **Daily Lessons** cover a variety of things. They go chronologically through the book usually with a pre-reading look at vocabulary and the study questions followed by the reading of the assigned section. After the reading is completed, you can check comprehension with the multiple choice questions if you like, then delve into the text looking at various elements of fiction as well as some items to build background knowledge. We've really tried to hit a variety of reading, language arts, and life skills throughout the unit.

Following the Daily Lessons are a series of lessons covering the **elements of fiction** for the book as a whole.

After the lessons for the elements of fiction, there are **reviewing/testing resources**. This section has multiple versions of seven different types of test parts: Matching, Fill in the Blanks, Short Answer, Extended Answer, Quotes, Multiple Choice, and Vocabulary. They are formatted for ease of use in mixing and matching, so you can choose the parts you want. Remember, we also have the Create Your Own Test feature on our website (www.tpet.com) where you can choose our questions and/or add your own to quickly and easily create tests, quizzes, and worksheets.

In the upper-elementary and middle school titles, we've included pages that are white-board friendly for **vocabulary** as well as the traditional worksheet format that is in the earlier editions of the LitPlans, with Part I: Contextual Clues and Part II: Matching the Definitions.

The **Short Answer study questions** are scattered throughout the unit, in with the appropriate Daily Lessons, but a complete set is also in the Additional Resources (after the Unit Tests) in case you prefer to have them all together. The **Multiple Choice questions** for comprehension quizzes and **Vocabulary Worksheets** can also be found there.

I hope you like the new LitPlans CT Edition! Your feedback is always appreciated.

Mary

Mary Collins
Owner & Founder of Teacher's Pet Publications

TABLE OF CONTENTS
Dear Mr. Henshaw

- 7   **Overview: Objectives and CCSS Correlations**
- 18   **About The Author**
- 20   **Reading Assignments**
- **Daily Lessons**
  - 21   Lesson One: Beverly Cleary
  - 24   Lesson Two: Genre, Fiction, Diary
  - 25   Lesson Three: Vocabulary 1, Reading Assignment (RA) 1
  - 31   Lesson Four: Oral Reading Evaluations
  - 33   Lesson Five: Critical Thinking, Passages from RA 1
  - 37   Lesson Six: Vocabulary 2, Informational Reading, RA 2
  - 44   Lesson Seven: Review RA 2; Character Study of Leigh
  - 48   Lesson Eight: Vocabulary Review; RA 3
  - 55   Lesson Nine: Review RA 3; Map Skills; Inferences; Creative Closings
  - 61   Lesson Ten: Shoe Song Poem; Symbolism; Similes
  - 62   Lesson Eleven: Main Ideas RA 4; Christmas
  - 67   Lesson Twelve: RA5; Pseudonyms; Mr. Findley; Dialogue
  - 74   Lesson Thirteen: Vocabulary; RA 6;
  - 80   Lesson Fourteen: Inference; Bear Story Symbolism; Book Awards
  - 84   Lesson Fifteen: Review; RA 7
  - 96   Lesson Sixteen: Main Ideas RA 7; Narrative Writing
  - 99   Lesson Seventeen: RA 8; Character Development of Leigh
  - 104   Lesson Eighteen: Vocabulary; RA 9; Monarch Butterflies
  - 110   Lesson Nineteen: Review RA 9; Vocabulary RA 10
  - 120   Lesson Twenty: RA 10; Symbolism; Allusion
  - 126   Lesson Twenty-One: RA 11; Group Work, Main Idea
  - 127   Lesson Twenty-Two: RA 12; Discussion
  - 133   Character Lesson
  - 135   Theme Lesson
  - 136   Conflict Lesson
  - 138   Plot Lesson
  - 139   Symbolism Lesson

Dear Mr. Henshaw Table of Contents Page 2

Unit Review/Test Resources
    141   Matching
    147   Fill In The Blanks
    153   Short Answer
    164   Extended Answer
    167   Quotes
    171   Multiple Choice
    178   Vocabulary

Additional Resources
    184   Short Answer Study Questions
    186   Multiple Choice Questions
    199   Vocabulary Worksheets
    212   Quotations
    214   Bulletin Board Ideas
    215   Extra Activities
    216   Related Topics
    217   Unit Word List
    218   Unit Word Searches
    220   Unit Crossword
    222   Vocabulary Word List
    223   Vocabulary Word Searches
    227   Vocabulary Crossword

NOTES
Dear Mr. Henshaw

OVERVIEW: OBJECTIVES AND COMMON CORE CORRELATIONS
Dear Mr. Henshaw

DAILY LESSONS

Lesson One
1. Students will learn about Beverly Cleary, author of *Dear Mr. Henshaw*.
2. Students will practice listening skills while viewing a video about Beverly Cleary.
   CCSS Grade 4:
   CCSS Grade 5: RI.5.7,
   CCSS Grade 6: RI.6.7
3. Students will work in small groups to discuss the video.
   CCSS Grade 4: SL.4.1, SL.4.2, SL.4.3
   CCSS Grade 5: SL.5.1, SL.5.2, SL.5.3
   CCSS Grade 6: SL.6.1, SL.6.2
4. Students will be assigned a Beverly Cleary book for outside reading during this unit.
   CCSS Grade 4: RL.4.10
   CCSS Grade 5: RL.5.10
   CCSS Grade 6: RL.6.10

Lesson Two
1. Students will review and understand the meaning of "fiction."
2. Students will review the meaning of "genre" as it applies to fiction.
3. Students will discuss genres of literature and give examples of each.
   CCSS Grade 4:
   CCSS Grade 5: RL.5.9
   CCSS Grade 6: RL.6.9
4. Students will learn what a "diary" is and how that is relevant to *Dear Mr. Henshaw*.
5. Students will receive books and materials for the unit.

CCSS Note: This lesson is more of an introduction to or review of the literary terms of *fiction, nonfiction, genre,* and *diary* than a comparison of stories from the same genre; however, reviewing these terms and the various genres of literature will give students background knowledge for when they do make the comparisons.

Lesson Three
1. Students will preview vocabulary words for Reading Assignment 1 *(amuse, diorama, autographed)* so they have a better understanding of the words when the encounter them in the text.
   CCSS Grade 4: L.4.4, L.4.5, L.4.6
   CCSS Grade 5: L.5.4, L.5.5, L.5.6
   CCSS Grade 6: L.6.4, L.6.5, L.6.6

2. Students will preview the study questions for Reading Assignment 1 to get an idea of what things will be important in the upcoming reading assignment.
3. Students will read assigned entries from *Dear Mr. Henshaw* and predict what they think happened previously and what might happen next.
    CCSS Grade 4: RF.4.3, RF.4.4, RL.4.10
    CCSS Grade 5: RL.5.10
    CCSS Grade 6: RL.5.10

Lesson Four
1. Students will review the introductory lesson materials.
2. Students will read orally and have their reading evaluated.
    CCSS Grade 4: RF.4.3, RF.4.4, RL.4.10
    CCSS Grade 5: RL.5.10
    CCSS Grade 6: RL.6.10
3. Students will complete Reading Assignment 1.

Lesson Five
1. Students will review the main events and ideas from Reading Assignment 1.
2. Students will practice critical thinking skills while discussing point of view, motive, and personal relationships based on selected passages or events from Reading Assignment 1.
    CCSS Grade 4: RL.4.1, RL.4.2, RL.4.3, RL.4.6, L.4.5b, SL.4.1
    CCSS Grade 5: RL.5.1, RL.5.6, RI.5.2, SL.5.1
    CCSS Grade 6: RL.6.1, RL.6.3, RL.6.4, RL.6.6, SL.6.1

Lesson Six
1. Students will preview the vocabulary for Reading Assignment 2: *according, nagging, hauling,* and *barreling*.
    CCSS Grade 4: L.4.4, L.4.5, L.4.6
    CCSS Grade 5: L.5.4, L.5.5, L.5.6
    CCSS Grade 6: L.6.4, L.6.5, L.6.6
2. Students will preview the study questions for Reading Assignment 2 of and predict what they think will happen based on the questions that are asked.
3. Students will read Reading Assignment 2 of *Dear Mr. Henshaw*.
    CCSS Grade 4: RF.4.3, RF.4.4, RL.4.10
    CCSS Grade 5: RL.5.10
    CCSS Grade 6: RL.5.10

Dear Mr. Henshaw Overview & CCSS Correlations Page 3

4. Students will have their oral reading evaluated.
   CCSS Grade 4: RF.4.3, RF.4.4, RL.4.10
   CCSS Grade 5: RL.5.10
   CCSS Grade 6: RL.6.10
5. Students will investigate California's Central Valley, California's Central Coast, Taft, Bakersfield, Pacific Grove, and Interstate 5 to read informational texts and practice map reading skills.
   CCSS Grade 4: RI.4.1, RI.4.2, RI.4.10
   CCSS Grade 5: RI.5.1, RI.5.2, RI.5.4, RI.5.7, RI.5.10
   CCSS Grade 6: RI.6.1, RI.6.2, RI.6.4, RI.6.7, RI.6.10

Lesson Seven
1. Students will review the main ideas and events of Reading Assignment 2.
   CCSS Grade 4: RL.4.1, RL.4.10
   CCSS Grade 5: RL.5.1, RL.5.10
   CCSS Grade 6: RL.6.1, RL.6.4, RL.6.10
2. Students will study the character of Leigh through his answers to Mr. Henshaw's questions.
   CCSS Grade 4: RL.4.3, RL.4.1, RL.4.4, RL.4.10
   CCSS Grade 5: RL.5.1, RL.5.4, RL.5.10
   CCSS Grade 6: RL.6.1, RL.6.4, RL.6.10
3. Students will compose a poem using adjectives describing Leigh.
   CCSS Grade 4: RL.4.3, RL.4.5, W.4.10, L.4.3
   CCSS Grade 5: W.5.10, L.5.3b
   CCSS Grade 6: W.6.10,
4. Students will write answers to Mr. Henshaw's questions as they pertain to themselves.
   CCSS Grade 4: W.4.2, W.4.4, W.4.5, W.4.10
   CCSS Grade 5: W.5.2, W.5.4, W.5.5, W.5.10
   CCSS Grade 6: W.6.2, W.6.4, W.6.5, W.6.10
5. Students will share the information about themselves with each other.

Lesson Eight
1. Students will review vocabulary words and characters previously introduced.
2. Students will preview the vocabulary words (*rude, refinery, nuisance*) and study questions for Reading Assignment 3 (December 4-December 21).
   CCSS Grade 4: L.4.4, L.4.5, L.4.6
   CCSS Grade 5: L.5.4, L.5.5, L.5.6
   CCSS Grade 6: L.6.4, L.6.5, L.6.6
3. Students will read Reading Assignment 3.
   CCSS Grade 4: RF.4.3, RF.4.4, RL.4.10
   CCSS Grade 5: RL.5.10
   CCSS Grade 6: RL.5.10

Lesson Nine
1. Students will review the main ideas and events from Reading Assignment 3.
   CCSS Grade 4: RL.4.1, RL.4.10
   CCSS Grade 5: RL.5.1, RL.5.10
   CCSS Grade 6: RL.6.1, RL.6.4, RL.6.10
2. Students will learn about the idiom "where he hangs his hat."
   CCSS Grade 4: RL.4.1, L.4.5b
   CCSS Grade 5: RL.5.1
   CCSS Grade 6: RL.6.1
3. Students will learn more about refineries, canapes, quiche, and partitions.
   CCSS Grade 4: RI.4.1, RI.4.2, RI.4.10
   CCSS Grade 5: RI.5.1, RI.5.2, RI.5.4, RI.5.7, RI.5.10
   CCSS Grade 6: RI.6.1, RI.6.2, RI.6.4, RI.6.7, RI.6.10
4. Students will locate Wyoming and Alaska on a map and compare & contrast the flags of these states.
5. Students will explore one example of making inferences from the written text.
   CCSS Grade 4: RL.4.1, L.4.5b
   CCSS Grade 5: RL.5.1
   CCSS Grade 6: RL.6.1
6. Students will examine the creative closings Leigh uses and connect the closings with the ideas, events, or sentiments expressed in the corresponding letters.
7. Students will preview the vocabulary words (*quilted, fictitious*) and study questions for Reading Assignment 4 and complete the reading prior to the next class meeting.
   CCSS Grade 4: L.4.4, L.4.5, L.4.6
   CCSS Grade 5: L.5.4, L.5.5, L.5.6
   CCSS Grade 6: L.6.4, L.6.5, L.6.6

Lesson Ten
1. Students will make up a "shoe song" (poem) like the ones in the December 24th entry.
   CCSS Grade 4: RL.4.3, RL.4.5, W.4.10
   CCSS Grade 5: W.5.10, L.5.3b
   CCSS Grade 6: W.6.10
2. Students will explore the idea of the "lost shoe" as being symbolic of divorce.
   CCSS Grade 4: RL.4.1, L.4.5b
   CCSS Grade 5: RL.5.1
   CCSS Grade 6: RL.6.1
3. Students will learn about similes, using the comparison of a divorced person to a lost shoe.
   CCSS Grade 4: RL.4.1, L.4.5a
   CCSS Grade 5: RL.5.1
   CCSS Grade 6: RL.6.1
4. Students will think of other similes that describe divorce and create a bulletin board with their ideas.

Dear Mr. Henshaw Overview & CCSS Correlations Page 5

Lesson Eleven
1. Students will review the main ideas and events from Reading Assignment 4.
   CCSS Grade 4: RL.4.1, RL.4.10
   CCSS Grade 5: RL.5.1, RL.5.10
   CCSS Grade 6: RL.6.1, RL.6.4, RL.6.10
2. Students will discuss Christmas traditions and share what they know about this holiday.
   CCSS Grade 4: SL.4.1
   CCSS Grade 5: SL.5.1
   CCSS Grade 6: SL.6.1
3. Students will write to inform and describe in an essay entitled, "My Perfect Christmas."
   CCSS Grade 4: W.4.2, W.4.4, W.4.5, W.4.10
   CCSS Grade 5: W.5.2, W.5.4, W.5.5, W.5.10
   CCSS Grade 6: W.6.2, W.6.4, W.6.5, W.6.10

Lesson Twelve
1. Students will preview the study questions for Reading Assignment 5.
2. Students will read Reading Assignment 5.
   CCSS Grade 4: RF.4.3, RF.4.4, RL.4.10
   CCSS Grade 5: RL.5.10
   CCSS Grade 6: RL.5.10
3. Students will discuss the study questions for Reading Assignment 5.
   CCSS Grade 4: RL.4.1, RL.4.10
   CCSS Grade 5: RL.5.1, RL.5.10
   CCSS Grade 6: RL.6.1, RL.6.4, RL.6.10
4. Students will learn about pseudonyms, Hermiston Oregon, the Columbia River, and juke boxes.
   CCSS Grade 4: RI.4.1, RI.4.2, RI.4.10
   CCSS Grade 5: RI.5.1, RI.5.2, RI.5.4, RI.5.7, RI.5.10
   CCSS Grade 6: RI.6.1, RI.6.2, RI.6.4, RI.6.7, RI.6.10
5. Students will learn about figurative language--specifically, hyperboles.
   CCSS Grade 4: RL.4.4, L.4.5
   CCSS Grade 5: RL.5.4
   CCSS Grade 6: RL.6.4
6. Students will study Mr. Findley's character in more detail.
   CCSS Grade 4: RL.4.3, RL.4.1, RL.4.4, RL.4.10
   CCSS Grade 5: RL.5.1, RL.5.4, RL.5.10
   CCSS Grade 6: RL.6.1, RL.6.4, RL.6.10
7. Students will explore the idea of listening to and writing dialogue.
   CCSS Grade 4: W.4.3b, W.4.4, W.4.5, W.4.10
   CCSS Grade 5: W.5.3b, W.5.4, W.5.5, W.5.10
   CCSS Grade 6: W.6.3b, W.6.4, W.6.5, W.6.10

Dear Mr. Henshaw Overview & CCSS Correlations Page 6

Lesson Thirteen
1. Students will learn about the vocabulary words for Reading Assignment 6: *decided, hibernated, mimeograph,* and *nuisance*.
   CCSS Grade 4: L.4.4, L.4.5, L.4.6
   CCSS Grade 5: L.5.4, L.5.5, L.5.6
   CCSS Grade 6: L.6.4, L.6.5, L.6.6
2. Students will preview the study questions for Reading Assignment 6.
3. Students will read Reading Assignment 6.
   CCSS Grade 4: RF.4.3, RF.4.4, RL.4.10
   CCSS Grade 5: RL.5.10
   CCSS Grade 6: RL.5.10
4. Students will locate Yellowstone Park, Kansas, and Wyoming on a map and learn a little bit about Yellowstone.
   CCSS Grade 4: RI.4.1, RI.4.2, RI.4.10
   CCSS Grade 5: RI.5.1, RI.5.2, RI.5.4, RI.5.7, RI.5.10
   CCSS Grade 6: RI.6.1, RI.6.2, RI.6.4, RI.6.7, RI.6.10

Lesson Fourteen
1. Students will discuss and answer the study questions for Reading Assignment 6.
   CCSS Grade 4: RL.4.1, RL.4.10
   CCSS Grade 5: RL.5.1, RL.5.10
   CCSS Grade 6: RL.6.1, RL.6.4, RL.6.10
2. Students will study a specific instance of inference in this assignment.
   CCSS Grade 4: RL.4.1, RL.4.4, RL.4.10
   CCSS Grade 5: RL.5.4, RL.5.10
   CCSS Grade 6: RL.6.4, RL.6.10
3. Students will discuss how Mr. Henshaw's bear story relates to Leigh's life.
   CCSS Grade 4: SL.4.1, SL.4.2, RL.4.10
   CCSS Grade 5: RL.5.1, RL.5.10, SL.5.1, SL.5.2
   CCSS Grade 6: RL.6.1, RL.6.10, SL.6.1, SL.6.2
4. Students will discuss the importance of doing what you say you will do.
   CCSS Grade 4: SL.4.1, SL.4.2
   CCSS Grade 5: SL.5.1, SL.5.2
   CCSS Grade 6: SL.6.1, SL.6.2
5. Students will learn about the Newbery Award and other book awards.

Dear Mr. Henshaw Overview & CCSS Correlations Page 7

Lesson Fifteen
1. Students will review information covered in reading assignments 3-6.
    CCSS Grade 4: RL.4.1, RL.4.10
    CCSS Grade 5: RL.5.1, RL.5.10
    CCSS Grade 6: RL.6.1, RL.6.4, RL.6.10
2. Students will preview the vocabulary words for Reading Assignment 7: *scowling, comfortable, ulcers, desert, wrath, mildew, receiver,* and *reception*.
    CCSS Grade 4: L.4.4, L.4.5, L.4.6
    CCSS Grade 5: L.5.4, L.5.5, L.5.6
    CCSS Grade 6: L.6.4, L.6.5, L.6.6
3. Students will preview the study questions for Reading Assignment 7.
4. Students will read Reading Assignment 7.
    CCSS Grade 4: RF.4.3, RF.4.4, RL.4.10
    CCSS Grade 5: RL.5.10
    CCSS Grade 6: RL.5.10

Lesson Sixteen
1. Students will discuss the Study Questions for Reading Assignment 7.
    CCSS Grade 4: RL.4.1, RL.4.10
    CCSS Grade 5: RL.5.1, RL.5.10
    CCSS Grade 6: RL.6.1, RL.6.4, RL.6.10
2. Students will work in small groups to determine the main events and ideas for Reading Assignment 7.
    CCSS Grade 4: SL.4.1, SL.4.2, RL.4.10
    CCSS Grade 5: RL.5.1, RL.5.10, SL.5.1, SL.5.2
    CCSS Grade 6: RL.6.1, RL.6.10, SL.6.1, SL.6.2
3. Students will write a narrative summarizing the important events and ideas for Reading Assignment 7.
    CCSS Grade 4: W.4.4, W.4.5, W.4.10
    CCSS Grade 5: W.5.4, W.5.5, W.5.10
    CCSS Grade 6: W.6.4, W.6.5, W.6.10

Lesson Seventeen
1. Students will read Reading Assignment 8.
    CCSS Grade 4: RF.4.3, RF.4.4, RL.4.10
    CCSS Grade 5: RL.5.10
    CCSS Grade 6: RL.5.10
2. Students will discuss the importance of Reading Assignment 8 in the context of the novel.
    CCSS Grade 4: SL.4.1, SL.4.2, RL.4.10
    CCSS Grade 5: RL.5.1, RL.5.10, SL.5.1, SL.5.2
    CCSS Grade 6: RL.6.1, RL.6.10, SL.6.1, SL.6.2

3. Students will discuss the development and growth of Leigh through this point in the book.
   CCSS Grade 4: RL.4.3, RL.4.10, SL.4.1, SL.4.2
   CCSS Grade 5: RL.5.1, SL.5.1, SL.5.2
   CCSS Grade 6: RL.6.1, SL.6.1, SL.6.2

Lesson Eighteen
1. Students will preview the vocabulary words for Reading Assignment 9: *antique, molest, quivering*, and *weird*.
   CCSS Grade 4: L.4.4, L.4.5, L.4.6
   CCSS Grade 5: L.5.4, L.5.5, L.5.6
   CCSS Grade 6: L.6.4, L.6.5, L.6.6
2. Students will preview the study questions for Reading Assignment 9.
3. Students will read Reading Assignment 9.
   CCSS Grade 4: RF.4.3, RF.4.4, RL.4.10
   CCSS Grade 5: RL.5.10
   CCSS Grade 6: RL.5.10
4. Students will view a short video about Monarch butterflies and write a descriptive paragraph.
   CCSS Grade 4: W.4.4, W.4.5, W.4.10
   CCSS Grade 5: W.5.4, W.5.5, W.5.10
   CCSS Grade 6: W.6.4, W.6.5, W.6.10

Lesson Nineteen
1. Students will review the main events and ideas from Reading Assignment 9.
   CCSS Grade 4: RL.4.1, RL.4.10
   CCSS Grade 5: RL.5.1, RL.5.10
   CCSS Grade 6: RL.6.1, RL.6.4, RL.6.10
2. Students will review literary genres.
3. Students will preview the vocabulary words for Reading Assignment 10: *villains, grateful, insulated, fastening, demonstration, muffle*, and *prowls*.
   CCSS Grade 4: L.4.4, L.4.5, L.4.6
   CCSS Grade 5: L.5.4, L.5.5, L.5.6
   CCSS Grade 6: L.6.4, L.6.5, L.6.6
4. Students will preview the Study Questions for and read Reading Assignment 10.
   CCSS Grade 4: RF.4.3, RF.4.4, RL.4.10
   CCSS Grade 5: RL.5.10
   CCSS Grade 6: RL.5.10

Dear Mr. Henshaw Overview & CCSS Correlations Page 9

Lesson Twenty
1. Students will review the main events and ideas from Reading Assignment 10.
   CCSS Grade 4: RL.4.1, RL.4.10
   CCSS Grade 5: RL.5.1, RL.5.10
   CCSS Grade 6: RL.6.1, RL.6.4, RL.6.10
2. Students will discuss the symbolism of Leigh's wax man.
   CCSS Grade 4: SL.4.1, SL.4.2, RL.4.10
   CCSS Grade 5: RL.5.1, RL.5.10, SL.5.1, SL.5.2
   CCSS Grade 6: RL.6.1, RL.6.10, SL.6.1, SL.6.2
3. Students will learn about allusion and explore the allusion in the March 15th entry.
   CCSS Grade 4: RL.4.4, L.4.5
   CCSS Grade 5: RL.5.4
   CCSS Grade 6: RL.6.4
4. Students will discuss Leigh's difficulty with endings in this section of the book.
   CCSS Grade 4: SL.4.1, SL.4.2, RL.4.10
   CCSS Grade 5: RL.5.1, RL.5.10, SL.5.1, SL.5.2
   CCSS Grade 6: RL.6.1, RL.6.10, SL.6.1, SL.6.2
5. Students will compare the adult male characters in *Dear Mr. Henshaw*.
   CCSS Grade 4: RL.4.3, SL.4.1, SL.4.2
   CCSS Grade 5: RL.5.3, SL.5.1, SL.5.2
   CCSS Grade 6: RL.6.1, SL.6.1, SL.6.2
6. Students will explore one way of creating descriptive sentences.
   CCSS Grade 4: RL.4.1, RL.4.2
   CCSS Grade 5: RL.5.1, RL.5.4
   CCSS Grade 6: RL.6.1, RL.6.4
7. Students will practice quick-writing on a number of different topics.
   CCSS Grade 4: W.4.10
   CCSS Grade 5: W.5.10
   CCSS Grade 6: W.6.10
8. Students will review the vocabulary words introduced so far in this unit.

Lesson Twenty-One
1. Students will read Reading Assignment 11 in class.
   CCSS Grade 4: RF.4.3, RF.4.4, RL.4.10
   CCSS Grade 5: RL.5.10
   CCSS Grade 6: RL.5.10
2. Students will collaborate to determine and discuss the most important events in this section of the book.
   CCSS Grade 4: RL.4.1, RL.4.10
   CCSS Grade 5: RL.5.1, RL.5.10
   CCSS Grade 6: RL.6.1, RL.6.4, RL.6.10

Copyright 2014

3. Students will determine the main ideas in each dated entry of Reading Assignment and create one study question for each main idea.
   CCSS Grade 4: SL.4.1, SL.4.2, RL.4.10
   CCSS Grade 5: RL.5.1, RL.5.10, SL.5.1, SL.5.2
   CCSS Grade 6: RL.6.1, RL.6.10, SL.6.1, SL.6.2
4. Students will lead a class discussion and take notes for studying purposes.
   CCSS Grade 4: SL.4.1, SL.4.2, RL.4.10
   CCSS Grade 5: RL.5.1, RL.5.10, SL.5.1, SL.5.2
   CCSS Grade 6: RL.6.1, RL.6.10, SL.6.1, SL.6.2
5. Prior to the next class meeting, students will read Reading Assignment 12.
   CCSS Grade 4: RF.4.3, RF.4.4, RL.4.10
   CCSS Grade 5: RL.5.10
   CCSS Grade 6: RL.5.10

Lesson Twenty-Two
1. Students will review the main ideas and events from Reading Assignment 12.
   CCSS Grade 4: RL.4.1, RL.4.10
   CCSS Grade 5: RL.5.1, RL.5.10
   CCSS Grade 6: RL.6.1, RL.6.4, RL.6.10
2. Students will discuss several passages from Reading Assignment 12 to gain a better understanding of the characters and themes.
   CCSS Grade 4: SL.4.1, SL.4.2, RL.4.10
   CCSS Grade 5: RL.5.1, RL.5.10, SL.5.1, SL.5.2
   CCSS Grade 6: RL.6.1, RL.6.10, SL.6.1, SL.6.2

ADDITIONAL LESSONS
Character
CCSS Grade 4: RL.4.1, RL.4.3, RL.4.4, SL.4.1, SL.4.2
CCSS Grade 5: RL.5.1, RL.5.3, SL.5.1, SL.5.2
CCSS Grade 6: RL.6.1, RL.6.3, SL.6.1, SL.6.2

Theme
CCSS Grade 4: RL.4.2, RL.4.4, SL.4.1, SL.4.2
CCSS Grade 5: RL.5.1, RL.5.2, RL.5.4, SL.5.1, SL.5.2
CCSS Grade 6: RL.6.1, RL.6.2, RL.6.4, SL.6.1, SL.6.2

Conflict
CCSS Grade 4: RL.4.1, RL.4.4, SL.4.1, SL.4.2
CCSS Grade 5: RL.5.1, RL.5.4, SL.5.1, SL.5.2
CCSS Grade 6: RL.6.1, RL.6.4, SL.6.1, SL.6.2

Dear Mr. Henshaw Overview & CCSS Correlations Page 11

Plot
CCSS Grade 4: RL.4.1, RL.4.4, SL.4.1, SL.4.2
CCSS Grade 5: RL.5.1, RL.5.4, RL.5.5, SL.5.1, SL.5.2
CCSS Grade 6: RL.6.1, RL.6.3, RL.6.4, RL.6.5, SL.6.1, SL.6.2

Symbolism
CCSS Grade 4: RL.4.1, RL.4.4, SL.4.1, SL.4.2
CCSS Grade 5: RL.5.1, RL.5.4, SL.5.1, SL.5.2
CCSS Grade 6: RL.6.1, RL.6.4, SL.6.1, SL.6.2

ADDITIONAL RESOURCES
Vocabulary Worksheets
CCSS Grade 4: RL.4.4, L.4.4a, L.4.4b
CCSS Grade 5: RL.5.4, L.5.4a, L.5.4b
CCSS Grade 6: RL.6.4

A FEW NOTES ABOUT THE AUTHOR
Beverly Cleary

BEVERLY CLEARY is one of America's most popular authors. Born in McMinnville, Oregon, she lived on a farm in Yamhill until she was six and then moved to Portland. After college, she became the children's librarian in Yakima, Washington. In 1940, she married Clarence T. Cleary, and they are the parents of twins, now grown.

Mrs. Cleary's books have earned her many prestigious awards, including the American Library Association's Laura Ingalls Wilder Award, presented in recognition of her lasting contribution to children's literature. Her Dear Mr. Henshaw was awarded the 1984 John Newbery Medal, and her Ramona and Her Father and Ramona Quimby, Age 8 have been named Newbery Honor Books. In addition, her books have won more than thirty statewide awards based on the votes of her young readers.

Her characters such as Henry Huggins, Ellen Tebbits, Otis Spofford, Beezus and Ramona Quimby, as well as Ribsy, Socks, and Ralph S. Mouse, have delighted children for more than a generation.

Major Works

Henry Huggins, 1950
Ellen Tebbits, 1951
Henry and Beezus, 1952
Otis Spofford 1953
Henry and Ribsy, 1954
Beezus and Ramona, 1955
Fifteen, 1956
Henry and the Paper Route. 1957
The Luckiest Girl, 1958
Jean and Johnny, 1959
The Hullabaloo ABC, 1960
The Real Hole, 1960
Beaver and Wally, 1960
Here's Beaver!, 1961
Two Dog Biscuits, 1961
Emily's Runaway Imagination, 1961
Henry and the Clubhouse, 1962
Sister of the Bride, 1963
Ribsy, 1964
The Mouse and the Motorcycle, 1965
The Growing-Up Feet, 1967
Mitch and Amy, 1967

Ramona the Pest, 1968
Runaway Ralph, 1970
Socks, 1973
Ramona the Brave, 1975
Ramona and Her Father, 1977
Ramona and Her Mother, 1979
Ramona Quimby, Age 8, 1981
Ralph S. Mouse, 1982
Dear Mr. Henshaw, 1983
Ramona Forever, 1984
The Ramona Quimby Diary, 1984
Lucky Chuck, 1984
Janet's Thingamajigs, 1987
A Girl from Yamhill, 1988
Muggie Maggie, 1990
Strider, 1991
Petey's Bedtime Story, 1993
My Own Two Feet, 1995
Ramona's World, 1999

Awards
1978 Newbery Honor Book, Ramona and Her Father
1982 Newbery Honor Book, Ramona Quimby, Age 8
1984 Newbery Medal, Dear Mr. Henshaw
National Book Award, Ramona and Her Mother
Catholic Library Association's 1980 Regina Medal Award
University of Southern Mississippi's 1982 Silver Medallion
Children's Book Council 1985 Everychild Award
American Library Association's 1975 Laura Ingalls Wilder Award
Named a 2000 Library of Congress "Living Legend"

READING ASSIGNMENT SHEET
Dear Mr. Henshaw

Page numbers reference the text ISBN 9780380709588

Assignment	Pages: Dates	Read By
Reading Assignment 1	1-13: May 12 - November 16	
Reading Assignment 2	14-30: November 20 - December 1	
Reading Assignment 3	31-37: December 4 - December 21	
Reading Assignment 4	38-44: December 22 - December 25	
Reading Assignment 5	45-53: January 3 - January 10	
Reading Assignment 6	54-59: January 12 - January 19	
Reading Assignment 7	61-72: January 20 - February 4	
Reading Assignment 8	73-78: February 5	
Reading Assignment 9	79-87: February 6 - February 9	
Reading Assignment 10	89-104: February 15 - March 15	
Reading Assignment 11	104-111: March 16 - March 24	
Reading Assignment 12	111-134: March 25 - March 31 (end of book)	

LESSON ONE
Dear Mr. Henshaw

Objectives
    1. Students will learn about Beverly Cleary, author of *Dear Mr. Henshaw*.
    2. Students will practice listening skills while viewing a video about Beverly Cleary.
    3. Students will work in small groups to discuss the video.
    4. Students will be assigned a Beverly Cleary book for outside reading during this unit.

Activity 1
Show students a video interview with Beverly Cleary. This one is about 15 minutes long:
https://www.youtube.com/watch?v=6b0fY9SmqDY

With this lesson, there is a listening guide students can fill out while watching the video. Students should get together after the video to compare answers and talk about the video. Come together as a class to discuss the video and the correct answers.

Activity 2
Share with students a list of books written by Beverly Cleary. (One is provided at the beginning of this manual.) Have as many as possible available in your classroom for students to look at and read. Have each book name on a colorful piece of paper (folded up) in a hat or box. Let each student pick out one piece of paper, one book title, to read as outside reading during this unit.

Ask if anyone has already read the book they have pulled from the hat. If so, let students exchange with another student.

Let each student say the name of his/her book out loud. Discuss the impressive number of books Beverly Cleary has written.

At the end of the unit, on the day after the unit test, come back together as a class to discuss the books...what they are about, how they may be similar or different from each other...and what we can learn about Beverly Cleary from the characteristics of her books. You may have students create their own book covers for their outside reading Beverly Cleary books, and post them on a bulletin board or wall in your classroom—or make them into mobiles to hang in your room.

LISTENING GUIDE: BEVERLY CLEARY INTERVIEW

1. What is the biggest joy Beverly Cleary received from writing her books?

2. Of all her characters, who would Beverly Cleary like to have dinner with? Why?

3. How did Beverly Cleary come up with the character of Ramona?

4. Why do readers like Ramona?

5. Where does Beverly Cleary get ideas for her books?

6. Does Beverly Cleary write at a certain time every day?

7. What does D.E.A.R. stand for?

8. In what grade did Beverly Cleary discover she enjoyed reading?

LISTENING GUIDE: BEVERLY CLEARY INTERVIEW
ANSWER KEY

1. What is the biggest joy Beverly Cleary receives from writing her books?
   She enjoys the letters she gets from parents and children telling about someone who didn't like to read until reading one of her books.

2. Of all her characters, who would Beverly Cleary like to have dinner with? Why?
   She would like to have dinner with Ellen Tebbits because Ellen is the most mannerly of her characters.

3. How did Beverly Cleary come up with the character of Ramona?
   Someone outside in the neighborhood called the name Ramona while she was trying to decide what to name the character. Ramona was roughly based on a little girl in her neighborhood.

4. Why do readers like Ramona?
   Ramona does not learn to be a better little girl. She remains unreformed.

5. Where does Beverly Cleary get ideas for her books?
   She gets ideas from her own childhood, the childhood stories of others, the newspaper, and sometimes just out of thin air. In the case of *Dear Mr. Henshaw*, two boys asked her to write a story about a boy with divorced parents.

6. Does Beverly Cleary write at a certain time every day?
   For a long time, she would write just after breakfast, while baking bread, until lunchtime.

7. What does D.E.A.R. stand for?
   It stands for Drop Everything And Read.

8. In what grade did Beverly Cleary discover she enjoyed reading?
   She discovered it in the third grade.

LESSON TWO
Dear Mr. Henshaw

Objectives
1. Students will review and understand the meaning of "fiction."
2. Students will review the meaning of "genre" as it applies to fiction.
3. Students will discuss genres of literature and give examples of each.
4. Students will learn what a "diary" is and how that is relevant to *Dear Mr. Henshaw*.
5. Students will receive books and materials for the unit.

Activity #1
Discuss with students the meaning of the word "genre" as it applies to literature, then discuss the terms "fiction" and "non-fiction." You can search the Internet for a slideshare presentation about these terms to add a multimedia dimension to your presentation. Here is an example: http://www.slideshare.net/rdeable/genre-presentation-6833777 There are many others. Find one that suits your style.

Activity #2
After viewing the presentation, have students meet in small groups to answer these two questions:
- What are the main differences between fiction and non-fiction?
- What are some different types (genres) of fiction? List five and give examples of each.

Come back together as a class to discuss the answers.

Activity #3
Ask students, "What is a diary?" and find out if anyone in the class keeps a diary. Ask what elements go into a diary entry. After getting student responses, transition them into the explanation that diary entries often look a lot like a friendly letter, including a date, "Dear Diary," and the person's thoughts about recent happenings in his or her life.

Transition: Explain that *Dear. Mr. Henshaw*, written by Beverly Cleary, is a fictional book in the format of a collection of letters the main character (Leigh Botts) writes to Mr. Henshaw, his favorite author. Part way though the book, Leigh discovers that writing the letters is a good way to practice writing...and that he doesn't have to mail all the letters. When he discovers this, he still writes in a letter format, but because he doesn't mail all the letters, it turns into Leigh's diary.

Activity #4
Distribute the books and materials students will use during this unit.

LESSON THREE
Dear Mr. Henshaw

Objectives
1. Students will preview vocabulary words for Reading Assignment 1 so they have a better understanding of the words when they encounter them in the text.
2. Students will preview the study questions for Reading Assignment 1 to get an idea of what things will be important in the upcoming reading assignment.
3. Students will read assigned entries from *Dear Mr. Henshaw* and predict what they think happened previously and what might happen next.

Activity #1
Discuss the vocabulary words for the first reading assignment with your students. The vocabulary pages following this lesson are designed to be used with your whiteboard, but they could be printed and given to students if you so choose.

Activity #2
Preview the study questions for the first reading assignment with your students. The student pages (without answers) follow the vocabulary pages at the end of this daily lesson plan. The answer key follows Lesson Five, when the answers will be discussed in class.

Activity #3
Tell students they will each have the opportunity to read orally in class. Each student will be assigned a dated letter or diary entry to read. At the end of this lesson there is a schedule you can fill out to make the appropriate assignments. Tell students they should practice reading their passages. Make the assignments. Give students a few minutes to look up their passages and preview them.

Activity #4
Have students do a Quick Write giving their reaction to the passages they have been assigned. Ask them what they think happened in previous entries and what they think might happen after theirs.

Dear Mr. Henshaw
Vocabulary For Reading Assignment 1

AMUSE

The boy's father said city dogs were bored so Joe could not keep the dog unless he could think up seven ways to amuse it. (Page 2)

Circle the word you think means something like amuse:

wash   exercise   entertain   feed   keep it quiet

Make up a sentence with the word amuse.

_____

_____

If something is amusing, it is (choose one)

funny   sad   ugly   pretty   work

If someone is amused, they will probably (choose one)

cry   frown   smile   sleep

Dear Mr. Henshaw
Vocabulary For Reading Assignment 1

DIORAMA

I made a diorama of *Ways to Amuse a Dog*, the book I wrote to you about two times before. (Page 3)

Circle which one you think means something like diorama:

movie   3-D picture   cake   bulletin board

Make up a sentence with the word diorama.

_____

_____

Where would you most likely see a diorama?

in a museum

at the beach

in a restaurant

Dear Mr. Henshaw
Vocabulary For Reading Assignment 1

AUTOGRAPHED

Please send me a list of your books that you wrote, an autographed picture and a bookmark. (Page 8)

Circle the word you think means something like autographed.

framed   old   color   signed   recent

Make up a sentence with the word autographed.

_____

_____

If you had a baseball autographed by Babe Ruth, would it be more or less valuable than a baseball not autographed by him?

more valuable   less valuable

Place your autograph here:

_____

STUDY QUESTIONS
Dear Mr. Henshaw Reading Assignment 1

May 12 - November 16

1. Who is Mr. Henshaw?

2. Why does Leigh start writing letters to Mr. Henshaw?

3. Who is Bandit?

4. Why does Leigh read *Moose on Toast*?

5. What did Mr. Henshaw do that made Leigh angry?

6. Why does Leigh's mom feel that Leigh should answer the list of questions Mr. Henshaw sent?

7. Why does Leigh read *Ways to Amuse a Dog* so many times?

ORAL READING ASSIGNMENTS
Dear Mr. Henshaw

Page	Entry Date	Assigned To
2	December 3	
3	November 13	
4	December 2	
5	October 2	
6	November 7	
7	September 20	
9	November 15	
12	November 16	
14	November 20	
16	November 22	
18	November 23	
20	November 24	
23	November 26	
25	November 27	
27	December 1	
29	December 1, starting with *10. What do you wish?*	
31	December 4	
34	December 12	
36	December 13	
37	December 21	
39	December 22	
40	December 23	
41	December 24	
43	December 25	
45	January 3	

LESSON FOUR
Dear Mr. Henshaw

Objectives
1. Students will review the introductory lesson materials.
2. Students will read orally and have their reading evaluated.
3. Students will complete Reading Assignment 1.

Activity #1
Do a quick review of the information covered in the introductory lessons.
- Ask students what they remember about Beverly Cleary.
- Ask students the difference between fiction and non-fiction.
- Ask students to give you examples of some different kinds of literary genres.
- Review *amuse, diorama,* and *autographed.*

Activity #2
Begin reading *Dear Mr. Henshaw* orally. You read the first entry then have students read their assigned passages in chronological order. Complete an oral reading evaluation for each student as each passage is read.

A form for the evaluation follows in this lesson.

Oral reading of the book should continue until everyone has had a chance to read. After that, you should decide whether you want oral reading to continue (to give students the opportunity to practice and improve) or change to silent reading, paired reading, or group reading (or some combination of these options).

Try to complete reading through page 12 (November 16) today.

ORAL READING EVALUATION
Dear Mr. Henshaw

Name _____ Date _____

	Excellent	Good	Average	Fair	Poor
Fluency					
Clarity					
Audibility					
Pronunciation					
Expression					

Grade _____

Comments:

LESSON FIVE
Dear Mr. Henshaw

Objectives
1. Students will review the main events and ideas from Reading Assignment 1
2. Students will practice critical thinking skills while discussing point of view, motive, and personal relationships based on selected passages or events from Reading Assignment 1.

Activity #1
Give students a few minutes to look at and discuss the study questions for Reading Assignment 1. This can be done individually, in pairs, or in small groups–at your discretion. After students have had time to consider the questions and formulate answers, come together as a class to discuss the answers. The answer key to the study questions follows this daily lesson.

Activity #2
The study questions are questions students can find the answers to in the text. Follow up the discussion of the study questions with some or all of the Additional Points for Discussion & Activities, which require more critical thinking skills.

STUDY QUESTIONS ANSWER KEY
Dear Mr. Henshaw Reading Assignment 1

May 12 - November 16

1. Who is Mr. Henshaw?
    Mr. Henshaw is the author of Leigh's favorite book and the person to whom Leigh writes letters.

2. Why does Leigh start writing letters to Mr. Henshaw?
    Most of the beginning letters are related to school assignments; he writes to fulfill the requirements of a school assignment.

3. Who is Bandit?
    Bandit is Leigh's dog.

4. Why does Leigh read *Moose on Toast*?
    Leigh reads *Moose on Toast* because Mr. Henshaw apparently suggested Leigh should read a different book by him.

5. What did Mr. Henshaw do that made Leigh angry?
    Mr. Henshaw sent back funny answers to Leigh's questions and sent a list of questions for Leigh to answer.

6. Why does Leigh's mom feel that Leigh should answer the list of questions Mr. Henshaw sent?
    She says since Mr. Henshaw took the time to answer Leigh's questions, Leigh should take the time to answer Mr. Henshaw's.

7. Why does Leigh read *Ways to Amuse a Dog* so many times?
    His teacher reads it aloud to the class, and Leigh thinks it is funny. It is about a dog, which reminds him of his dog, Bandit. So, it becomes his favorite book which he uses for school assignments when given the option.

ADDITIONAL POINTS FOR DISCUSSION & ACTIVITIES
Dear Mr. Henshaw Reading Assignment 1

Point Of View:
Leigh writes, "I am the boy who wrote to you last year when I was in second grade."
- **Considering this sentence, what can you say about point of view?**
- Why did Leigh start his letter off this way? [He was probably told to start letters with an introduction, so he is introducing himself.]
- How many letters do you think Mr. Henshaw gets from his readers in a year?
- Is it likely Mr. Henshaw would remember Leigh's letter from last year?
- From Leigh's point of view, he is doing a good job of introducing himself and reminding Mr. Henshaw of a previous contact. However, from Mr. Henshaw's point of view, Leigh's letter was just one in a sea of letters he received last year.
- What this creates for us, the readers of Beverly Cleary's book, is humor. We are amused at a boy's naive comment because we know this isn't enough information for Mr. Henshaw to remember Leigh.

Motives:
On November 7 of Leigh's fifth grade year, he writes and tells Mr. Henshaw that he has taken Mr. Henshaw's suggestion and has read a different book, *Moose on Toast*.
Why did Mr. Henshaw suggest for Leigh to read a different one of his books?
Students may give many answers. Some possibilities are:
- Leigh has been writing to Mr. Henshaw about the same book in second grade, third grade, fourth grade, and now fifth grade. It appears as though this is the only book Leigh reads. Mr. Henshaw wants Leigh to grow as a reader and expand his reading list.
- Mr. Henshaw knows if Leigh enjoyed *Ways to Amuse a Dog*, he will probably also enjoy *Moose on Toast*.
- Mr. Henshaw wants to sell more books.
- Mr. Henshaw is tired of hearing about the same book all the time.

People have different motives for saying and doing the things they do. We should be aware of this and think about the possible reasons why they say and do what they do.

Personal Relationships, Reasoning:
Leigh sent Mr. Henshaw a list of questions to answer, yet he thinks that it is unfair of Mr. Henshaw to send *him* a list of questions.
- Was it fair of Leigh to send Mr. Henshaw a list of questions?
- Was it fair of Mr. Henshaw to send Leigh a list of questions?
- What does all of this suggest about personal relationships? What makes something "fair" or "not fair" when we interact with other people?

Dear Mr. Henshaw Additional Points For Discussion & Activities Reading Assignment 1 Page 2

- Are there times when doing something that is "not fair" is necessary? Under what circumstances could you ask a friend to do something extraordinary for you? Under what circumstances would a friend not mind doing something extraordinary for you?
- What would you suggest as some guidelines for building relationships with people?

Literal Versus Figurative:
Leigh writes, "If my dad were here, he'd tell you to go climb a tree."
What does "go climb a tree" mean?
Leigh means his dad would not expect him to answer Mr. Henshaw's questions.

LESSON SIX
Dear Mr. Henshaw

Objectives
1. Students will preview the vocabulary for Reading Assignment 2 of *Dear Mr. Henshaw*.
2. Students will preview the study questions for Reading Assignment 2 of *Dear Mr. Henshaw* and predict what they think will happen based on the questions that are asked.
3. Students will read Reading Assignment 2 of *Dear Mr. Henshaw*.
4. Students will have their oral reading evaluated.
5. Students will investigate California's Central Valley, California's Central Coast, Taft, Bakersfield, Pacific Grove, and Interstate 5 to read informational texts and practice map reading skills.

Activity #1
Preview the vocabulary for Reading Assignment 2 (November 20-December 1) with your students. The vocabulary pages following this daily lesson are intended for use with your whiteboard, but they may be copied and distributed to your students if you prefer.

Activity #2
Take a few minutes to read through the study questions for Reading Assignment 2 with your students. Ask them what they think will happen in the next section of the book, based on the questions that are asked. The study questions for Reading Assignment 2 follow the vocabulary pages at the end of this daily lesson. The answer key for the study questions is at the end of Lesson Seven.

Activity #3
Continue students' oral reading evaluations as students read their assigned passages through Reading Assignment 2 (November 20 - December 1).

Activity #4
After reading this section of the book, go onto the Internet with your class to explore information about California's Central Valley, California's Central Coast, Taft, Bakersfield, Pacific Grove, and Interstate 5.

Look the places up on maps and read a bit about them on Wikipedia or from some other source. You can do this as a whole class activity or if your school has computers for students, you can assign each item in the list to a small group of students, then come back together as a class and share the information.

The point is to explore the real places mentioned in the book, to have students read some informational texts, and to practice map reading skills. This could also be a homework assignment if all of your students have access to the Internet.

Dear Mr. Henshaw
Vocabulary For Reading Assignment 2

ACCORDING

"Now when the class lines up *according* to height, I am in the middle." (Page 15)

Circle the word you think means something like *according*.

without   determined by   around   inside   because of

"According to" is often used to cite a source, as in "*According* to my mom, I'm the best soccer player on our team." It is important to know the source of information you get so you can tell if the source is biased or prejudiced.

Make up a sentence with the word *according*.

_____

_____

According can also mean "in keeping with," as in: *According* to the baseball rules, you are out when you get three strikes.

FYI: "Accord" means *agreement*.

Dear Mr. Henshaw
Vocabulary For Reading Assignment 2

NAGGING

"Mom is nagging me about your dumb old questions." (Page 14)

Circle the word you think means something like nagging.

asking   helping   constantly reminding

No one likes to be nagged.
Someone who nags people often is called a nag or a nagger.

Make up a sentence with the word nagging.

_____

_____

Is it good to be a nag?

Are there times when you need to be nagged?

Dear Mr. Henshaw
Vocabulary For Reading Assignment 2

HAULING

"Dad used to drive for someone else, **hauling** stuff like cotton, sugar beets and other produce around Central California and Nevada." (Page 16)

Circle the word you think means something like **hauling**.

carrying   selling   picking   growing

Words have a dictionary meaning (*denotation*) and often a more specific meaning that is determined by usage over time (*connotation*).

Hauling's connotation is that the thing being transported is heavy; it's a hard load to move.

Make up a sentence with the word **hauling**.

_____

_____

Compare and contrast the words *hauling* and *dragging*.

Dear Mr. Henshaw
Vocabulary For Reading Assignment 2

BARRELING

"Instead of going straight to school, we'd go barreling along the freeway looking down on the tops of ordinary cars, then down the offramp and back to school just before the bell rang." (Page 29)

Circle the word you think means something like **barreling**.

creeping   poking   racing   speeding

Picture a big, old, wooden barrel—like ships used to carry or settlers used to hold rain water. What would happen if you would take one of those and roll it down a steep hill?
That's where the word barreling comes from.
The connotation of this word is that you're driving along fast and carefree.

Make up a sentence with the word **barreling**.

_____

_____

I don't often barrel down the highway because it's dangerous, but I know a teenage boy who frequently barrels along when he drives.

STUDY QUESTIONS
Dear Mr. Henshaw Reading Assignment 2

November 20 - December 1

1. Why does Leigh finally decide to write the answers to Mr. Henshaw's questions?

2. What does Leigh's dad do for a living? Why was that a problem for Leigh and his mother?

3. Leigh's mom is very busy. What are some of the things that she does?

4. Why do Leigh and his mom move from Bakersfield to Pacific Grove, California?

5. Why does Leigh's dad take Bandit?

6. Is Leigh a popular boy with the other students in his new school? Choose a sentence from the book to support your answer.

7. What are some of the things that bother Leigh?

8. What does Leigh tell Mr. Henshaw he wishes for about his dad?

Dear Mr. Henshaw STUDY QUESTIONS Reading Assignment 2 Page 2

9. Use this graphic organizer to make notes about Leigh's answers to Mr. Henshaw's questions.

What do you look like?	What is your family like?
Do you have any pets?	Do you like school?
Who are your friends?	Who is your favorite teacher?
What bothers you?	What do you wish?

LESSON SEVEN
Dear Mr. Henshaw

Objectives
1. Students will review the main ideas and events of Reading Assignment 2.
2. Students will study the character of Leigh through his answers to Mr. Henshaw's questions.
3. (Optional) Students will compose a poem using adjectives describing Leigh.
4. Students will write answers to Mr. Henshaw's questions as they pertain to themselves.
5. Students will share the information about themselves with each other.

Activity #1
Have students independently, in pairs, or in small groups discuss and respond to the study questions for the second reading assignment. When students have finished, come together as a whole class to review the answers. The answer key for the study questions follows this daily lesson.

Activity #3
Leigh calls himself "medium"–just an ordinary kid. Write the word ORDINARY BOY vertically on your board and ask students to come up with words or phrases describing Leigh, that start with each letter of the words "ordinary boy." Alternately, each letter of "ordinary boy" could just be a part of the word or phrase describing Leigh, rather than at the beginning.

Activity #4
Have prepared in advance a "booklet" for each of your students. Take 3 sheets of plain 8.5 x 11 paper stacked together and neatly fold them in half to make a booklet. Put 2 staples in the center to hold the booklet together.

- Give each student a "booklet."
- Explain to students that they are to create a book about themselves.
- They should each make a front cover that reflects their interests and or personality, including their names.
- They should number the inside pages 1, 2, 3, etc., through 10.
- On each page, at the top, they should write the question Mr. Henshaw asked Leigh. Question 1 goes on page 1, question 2 on page 2, and so on through the 10 questions.

- On each of the pages, then, students should answer the questions, telling about themselves.
- Each entry should be written in a friendly letter format, like Leigh's are.
- The back page should be blank.
- Tell students that when their booklets are completed, you will have a "book swap" at which time they will swap books with others in the class to learn more about each other. This will give them a "heads up" not to put anything too personal (that they don't want shared) into their booklets.

If students don't finish this assignment in class, they should complete it as homework. Be sure to tell students by when it needs to be completed. When the booklets are completed, have a booklet swap so students can read about each other. Post the completed booklets on the bulletin board or classroom walls.

STUDY QUESTIONS ANSWER KEY
Dear Mr. Henshaw Reading Assignment 2

November 20 - December 1

1. Why does Leigh finally decide to write the answers to Mr. Henshaw's questions?
    Leigh's mom says that if he really wants to become an author, he needs to write more--and answering the questions is the best way to get started. Since Leigh wants to become an author, he is motivated to answer the questions.

2. What does Leigh's dad do for a living? Why was that a problem for Leigh and his mother?
    Leigh's dad drives a truck around central California. Leigh and his mother didn't like it because he was gone too much.

3. Leigh's mom is very busy. What are some of the things that she does?
    She takes care of Leigh, works as a caterer, and goes to the community college.

4. Why do Leigh and his mom move from Bakersfield to Pacific Grove, California?
    Leigh's parents got a divorce, and his Mom wants to live near the ocean.

5. Why does Leigh's dad take Bandit?
    Leigh's dad takes Bandit because Leigh's mom says she cannot work and take care of Bandit. Also Leigh's dad likes to take Bandit in his truck because Bandit helps him stay awake on long hauls, and Bandit likes going because he gets bored staying alone at home.

6. Is Leigh a popular boy with the other students in his new school? Choose a sentence from the book to support your answer.
    Answers can vary, but the sentence chosen from the book should reflect that he is not popular with the other students. An example of a sentence would be: "I don't have a whole lot of friends in my new school" or "The kids here pay more attention to my lunch than they do to me." (page 25)

7. What are some of the things that bother Leigh?
    Leigh is bothered when someone steals something from his lunch bag, by having to walk to school slowly, by being left alone before school, by his father's not phoning, and by his father's calling him "kid."

8. What does Leigh tell Mr. Henshaw he wishes for about his dad?
    Leigh wishes his dad would give him a ride to school in his big rig, going a long route and getting there just before the bell rings.

Dear Mr. Henshaw STUDY QUESTIONS Reading Assignment 2 Page 2

9. Use this graphic organizer to make notes about Leigh's answers to Mr. Henshaw's questions.

What do you look like?
- "medium"
- no red hair
- not real big

What is your family like?
- mom & dad are divorced
- dad took the dog, Bandit, with him
- dad's a truck driver
- mom works for Catering by Katy & is studying to be a nurse

Do you have any pets?
- no pets
- had a dog, Bandit, stays with dad
- likes to ride in truck with dad
- no one home all day to care for a dog

Do you like school?
- It's ok.
- going means he can get out
- kids are there

Who are your friends?
- doesn't have any at school
- wishes some kids would ask him over

Who is your favorite teacher?
- doesn't have one
- likes Mr. Fridley, the custodian

What bothers you?
- having lunch stolen
- walking to school slowly
- lonely mornings
- dad's saying, "Keep your nose clean, kid"

What do you wish?
- someone would quit stealing lunch
- dad would show up & give him a ride to school in his rig

LESSON EIGHT
Dear Mr. Henshaw

Objectives
1. Students will review vocabulary words and characters previously introduced.
2. Students will preview the vocabulary words and study questions for Reading Assignment 3 (December 4-December 21).
3. Students will read Reading Assignment 3.

Activity #1
Have students complete the crossword puzzle *Dear Mr. Henshaw* Crossword 1 as a review of the vocabulary and some character information introduced in the first two reading assignments. Students could complete this individually, in pairs or small groups, or as a whole-class activity. Prepare the needed number of copies and distribute as needed, or use your interactive whiteboard for whole-class participation. If students complete the crossword individually or in small groups, check their answers together as a whole class.

Activity #2
Preview the vocabulary for Reading Assignment 3 (December 4-December 21) with your students. The vocabulary pages that follow this daily lesson are intended to be used with your whiteboard, but they may also be reproduced and distributed to your students if you prefer.

Activity #3
Take a few minutes to read through the study questions for Reading Assignment 3 with your students. Ask them what they think will happen in the next section of the book, based on the questions that are asked. Answers to the study questions follow Lesson Nine.

Activity #4
Continue students' oral reading evaluations as students read their assigned passages through this section of the book. Read through December 21.

REVIEW CROSSWORD 1
Dear Mr. Henshaw

Across
1. Leigh's favorite book: *Ways to Amuse a* ___
2. Leigh's dog
4. Another name for a tractor-trailer
7. To entertain
10. Henshaw book: ___ *on Toast*
11. Carrying or transporting
12. Leigh's favorite author

Down
1. 3-D scene
2. Speeding
3. Constant reminding or complaining
5. Signed
6. Determined by
8. State where Leigh lives
9. Classmates steal from his lunch.

REVIEW CROSSWORD 1 ANSWER KEY
Dear Mr. Henshaw

	1 D	O	G		2 B	A	3 N	D	I	T				
	I				A		A							
	O			4 R	I	G								
	R		5 A	R		G		6 A						
7 A	M	U	S	E		I		C		8 C				
M			T	L		N		C		A				
A			O	I		G		O		L				
			G	N				R		I				
			R	G				D		F				
			A			9 L		I		10 M	O	O	S	E
			P			E		N		O				
			11 H	A	U	L	I	N	G	R				
			E			G				N				
			D			12 H	E	N	S	H	A	W		

Across
1. Leigh's favorite book: *Ways to Amuse a* ___
2. Leigh's dog
4. Another name for a tractor-trailer
7. To entertain
10. Henshaw book: ___ *on Toast*
11. Carrying or transporting
12. Leigh's favorite author

Down
1. 3-D scene
2. Speeding
3. Constant reminding or complaining
5. Signed
6. Determined by
8. State where Leigh lives
9. Classmates steal from his lunch.

Dear Mr. Henshaw
Vocabulary For Reading Assignment 3

RUDE

"I am sorry I was rude in my last letter when I finished answering your questions." (Page 31)

Circle the word you think means something like rude.

colorful   having bad manners   sick   sad

Being rude is not very nice. When you are rude to someone, you may hurt their feelings or make them angry.

Make up a sentence with the word rude.

_____

_____

What might cause you to be rude to someone?

Dear Mr. Henshaw
Vocabulary For Reading Assignment 3

REFINERY

"I wish he still hauled sugar beets over to the refinery in Spreckels so he might come to see me." (Page 31)

Circle the word you think means something like refinery.

storage yard   grocery store   processing plant

We most often hear the word refinery associated with oil. Big oil refineries take crude oil and make it into gasoline, kerosine, and other products we can use. A beet refinery takes the beets and processes them to make some kinds of sugar. Sugar cane and maple sap are other things that are refined to make sweeteners–granulated sugar and maple syrup, respectively.

Make up a sentence with the word refinery.

_____

_____

Dear Mr. Henshaw
Vocabulary For Reading Assignment 3

NUISANCE

"I don't want to be a nuisance to you, but I wish you could tell me how." (Page 36)

Circle the word you think means something like nuisance.

relative   helper   pest   pen pal

Make up a sentence with the word nuisance.

_____

_____

What is something that you might do that would make you a nuisance to your teacher?

STUDY QUESTIONS
Dear Mr. Henshaw Reading Assignment 3

December 4 - December 21

1. Why is Leigh rude to Mr. Henshaw in his letter dated December 1?

2. Leigh has a problem with his lunch. What is it? How does Leigh feel about this? Why?

3. Mr. Fridley suggested Leigh should come to school a few minutes early every morning to do something. What does Mr. Fridley want Leigh to do?

4. Leigh has trouble with his first diary entries. What does Mr. Henshaw suggest that might help him get started?

LESSON NINE
Dear Mr. Henshaw

Objectives
1. Students will review the main ideas and events from Reading Assignment 3.
2. Students will learn about the idiom "where he hangs his hat."
3. Students will learn more about refineries, canapes, quiche, and partitions.
4. Students will locate Wyoming and Alaska on a map and compare & contrast the flags of these states.
5. Students will explore one example of making inferences from the written text.
6. Students will examine the creative closings Leigh uses and connect the closing with the ideas, events, or sentiments expressed in the corresponding letters.
7. Students will preview the vocabulary words and study questions for the next reading assignment and complete the reading prior to the next class meeting.

Activity #1
Discuss the answers to the study questions for Reading Assignment 3 together in class. The answer key follows this daily lesson.

Activity #2
The Additional Points For Discussion & Activities for Reading Assignment 3 (on the page following this daily lesson) would best be done with a little exploring on the Internet combined with class discussion. For the sake of time constraints, make your computer screen visible to all students. Follow the guidelines on the Additional Points for Discussion & Activities page.

Activity #3
Explain to students that the next reading section only has two vocabulary words: *quilted* and *fictitious*.

Explain to students what *quilted* means. Bring in some quilted fabric so they can see and feel it. Go to YouTube and search "Amish quilting bee." Play a short video that shows hand quilting and one that shows machine quilting. Ask if any students would like to learn more or to start an after-school quilting club.

Tell students that you have already discussed what fiction is (as opposed to non-fiction). Ask for a definition. Fiction has characters who are not real; they are made-up...and so are their names. If you wanted to convey the idea that a character's name is made up, how would you do it? Complete this sentence: Little Red Riding Hood is a _____ character. Some students may say "fiction." Introduce the word *fictitious* as an adjective that means something is made-up. Give other examples: a criminal using a fictitious name, the setting of a story being in a fictitious town.

Dear Mr. Henshaw Lesson Nine Continued

Assignment

Students should preview the study questions for Reading Assignment 4 (Friday, December 22 through Monday, December 25) and read that portion of the text prior to the next class meeting.

STUDY QUESTIONS ANSWER KEY
Dear Mr. Henshaw Reading Assignment 3

December 4 - December 21

1. Why is Leigh rude to Mr. Henshaw in his letter dated December 1?
    Leigh's dad forgets to send the December support payment and does not come to see him. Leigh is angry about that and takes it out on Mr. Henshaw.

2. Leigh has a problem with his lunch. What is it? How does Leigh feel about this? Why?
    Leigh's problem is that people keep stealing the good things out of his lunch. He is very upset by this because his mom puts special things like deviled eggs or sandwiches with good fillings spread all the way to the corners in his lunch. He wants all of his lunch at lunch time.

3. Mr. Fridley suggested Leigh should come to school a few minutes early every morning to do something. What does Mr. Fridley want Leigh to do?
    Mr. Fridley thinks Leigh should come early to help raise the flags.

4. Leigh has trouble with his first diary entries. What does Mr. Henshaw suggest that might help him get started?
    Mr. Henshaw suggests that Leigh should pretend that he is writing to someone.

ADDITIONAL POINTS FOR DISCUSSION & ACTIVITIES
Dear Mr. Henshaw Reading Assignment 3

1. Discuss the phrase "where he hangs his hat."
In the December 4th entry, Leigh says, "Mom tried to phone him at the trailer park where, as Mom says, he hangs his hat." Ask students what does "where he hangs his hat" mean? [It means the place where he lives.]

Share with students the background information that some men still wear hats (mostly baseball caps or knit caps in the winter) but prior to the 1970's almost all men wore hats. When they entered a building, it was polite to take off their hats–at which time they often hung them on a peg or hat rack. When the men came home from work, they would walk through the door and hang up their hats; thus, the phrase "where he hangs his hat" came to mean "home."

Ask students if they know anyone who usually wears a hat. Ask them how many different kinds of hats they can think of. Do a little exploration on the Internet to find pictures of different kinds of hats.

2. *Refinery* is one of the vocabulary words in this section of the book. While you're on the Internet, search for pictures of different kinds of refineries. If you have a refinery close by, you might schedule a field trip to see one "in person."

3. Canapes and quiche: Make (or have a parent make or buy) a quiche or some canapes to bring in for students to taste. Alternately, find some pictures of these food items on the Internet to show students what goodies (like stuffed mushrooms) Leigh got in his lunch. Maybe your cafeteria staff would be willing to create some of these items or some deviled eggs for you. Another idea is to have students bring in their parents' or grandparents', (or neighbor, etc.) recipe for deviled eggs. Compare recipes! Which sounds the best?

4. Although ***partition*** is not a vocabulary word, some students may not be familiar with it. Look for pictures of different kinds of partitions on the Internet. Does your school have any partitions? See if students know where they are.

5. Geography: Locate Wyoming and Alaska on the map. Find pictures of their state flags as well as the state flag for California (which Leigh helps to put up in the mornings). Compare and contrast the flags. Ask students why they think the flags' colors and pictures were chosen. Compare them to your state's flag. Discuss what a *halyard* is.

Dear Mr. Henshaw Additional Points for Discussion & Activities Reading Assignment 3 Continued

6. **Inferences:** How does Mr. Fridley know Leigh walks backwards to school? [watches him] How does Leigh's walking backwards make Mr. Fridley feel? [nervous] Would Mr. Fridley feel nervous about Leigh's walking backwards if he didn't care about Leigh? So, even though the text doesn't say Mr. Fridley cares about Leigh, we can *infer* that from what he says. Why do you think Mr. Fridley asks Leigh to help with the flags in the morning? [He can see that Leigh is lonesome and doesn't feel a part of things yet. Letting him help with the flags gives him something to do to contribute to the school community, makes him feel special (because not everyone gets to do this), and Mr. Fridley's taking an interest in him makes Leigh feel good ("It was nice to have somebody notice me.").] We can draw **inferences** from characters' actions and words to learn things that aren't directly stated.

7. **Closings**: Look back through Leigh's letters (not only in this section but back to the beginning of the book) and make a list of them. He's actually pretty creative in his closings. As you look back at the closings, ask students:

Date	Closing	Question
December 21	"Your grateful friend,"	For what is Leigh grateful?
December 13	"Puzzled reader,"	What puzzles Leigh?
December 4	"Still Your No. 1 Fan,"	Why did he close this way? (letter of apology?)
December 1	"Fooey on you,"	What's that mean? Why did Leigh say that?
November 26	"Pooped writer,"	What does "pooped" mean? Why is Leigh pooped?

Closings don't have to be only "sincerely" or "yours truly." They can be whatever you want them to be. Just be careful to match your closing to the situation in which you are writing.

STUDY QUESTIONS
Dear Mr. Henshaw Reading Assignment 4

December 22 - December 25

1. What are some of the ways that Leigh tries to keep people from stealing his lunch?

2. Since Leigh's dad did not spend Christmas with them the first year after the divorce, how does Leigh get his present?

LESSON TEN
Dear Mr. Henshaw

Objectives
1. Students will make up a "shoe song" (poem) like the ones in the December 24th entry.
2. Students will explore the idea of the "lost shoe" as being symbolic of divorce.
3. Students will learn about similes, using the comparison of a divorced person to a lost shoe.
4. Students will think of other similes that describe divorce and create a bulletin board with their ideas.

Activity #1
Review with students the shoe poems in the December 24th entry. Have students work in pairs to create their own lost shoe poems. Students should brainstorm ideas about lost shoes then turn those ideas into a poem. One way to start would be to think of all the words they can think of that rhyme with the word shoe. That will give them something concrete to work from. Give students ample time to complete this assignment, including writing their poems in big letters on a piece of colored construction paper to be posted on the bulletin board or classroom (or hallway) walls. Then, let students orally share their poems before posting them (or giving them to you to post). Vote on the best one(s) and put them up on your class's website.

Activity #2
After the fun from the poems settles down, ask students, "How is a lost shoe like a divorced person?" See what kinds of responses you get from your question and introduce the idea of the lost shoe as a *symbol* for a divorced person.

Explain that the phrase "a divorced person is like a lost shoe" is an example of a kind of figurative language called a *simile*. They can recognize a simile when they see two seemingly unlike things being compared by the words "like" or "as." Give some more examples of similes, then ask students to offer a few of their own.

Activity #3
- Have previously prepared a bulletin board or wall with blank paper (and maybe pictures or drawings of one of different kinds of shoes scattered over it). At the top write, "Divorce is like..." and "A divorced person (or family) is like...."
- Tell students to think of appropriate endings to these phrases. Remind them that divorce doesn't always make everyone unhappy. Sometimes things are better after a divorce, and to consider those circumstances as well when they are writing their endings.
- Allow small groups of students to go to the board (or wall) to write their endings. When all students have had a chance to write their endings, read and discuss them with the class.

LESSON ELEVEN
Dear Mr. Henshaw

Objectives:
1. Students will review the main ideas and events from Reading Assignment 4.
2. Students will discuss Christmas traditions and share what they know about this holiday.
3. Students will write to inform and describe in an essay entitled, "My Perfect Christmas." [Another holiday can be substituted if preferred.]

Activity #1
Discuss the answers to the study questions for Reading Assignment 4 together in class.

Activity #2
Leigh and his family celebrate Christmas. Take this opportunity to educate your students about what the holiday of Christmas actually is, share information about some traditional things some people do to celebrate this holiday, and to give students who celebrate Christmas the opportunity to tell what they do to celebrate it.

Note: Other holidays are celebrated in December, but the characters in *Dear Mr. Henshaw* celebrate Christmas. If you feel strongly that other holidays need to be represented, feel free to add your own insights and materials. This lesson deals only with Christmas because that is the holiday talked about in the book. For the writing assignment that follows, students may substitute their favorite holiday if they don't celebrate Christmas.

Ask students:
- What things do Leigh and his mom do for Christmas? [Leigh got a present from his dad, and Leigh and his mom ate dinner with Katy.]
- Why do people get and give gifts at Christmas? [The magi brought gifts for baby Jesus. It is the birth of Jesus Christ that is celebrated at Christmas; He is the "Christ" part of the word "Christmas."]
- Why do people gather together and eat a big dinner on Christmas? [Having a "feast" is an old-fashioned way of having a "party." People got together to eat and drink and celebrate the holiday.]
- Why would Katy host a dinner for women and their kids and a few old people? [People like Leigh and his mom and the others Katy invites don't have big families and lots of friends to "feast" with to celebrate the holiday—or perhaps don't have the means (money) to buy and prepare a feast for themselves. Katy is a kind woman who shares what she has.]

- What other traditions do you know that go with Christmas?
  [**Trees/Greens:** evergreens are a tradition from the European tradition, symbolizing new hope and life brought by Jesus and based in an older pagan tradition of celebrating the winter solstice with greens symbolizing life in the dead of winter and the hope of coming spring.
  Santa Claus and hanging stockings: based on St. Nicholas who delivered gifts to children & needed a place to leave them where the children would find them
  Wreaths: based on ancient European as well as Roman & Greek use, symbolizing strength or power and everlasting life (when made of evergreens)
  Singing Christmas Carols: began as early as the 4th century in Rome but more modern version developed in the 13th century in Europe
  Mistletoe: Druids believed mistletoe fell from heaven and grew onto a tree that sprang from Earth, thus representing the joining of heaven and Earth. According to Christian tradition, Jesus was both God and Man, making mistletoe an appropriate Christmas symbol/tradition.
  Holly: has sharp points like the crown of thorns Jesus wore, red berries symbolizing Christ's blood shed on the cross, and evergreen leaves symbolizing everlasting life
  Candy Canes: in the shape of J for Jesus, red symbolizing blood, white symbolizing purity
  There are many others students (or you) might suggest; these are just a few.
- We now have the "holiday season" which starts with Thanksgiving (some may say Halloween) and goes through New Year's Day. So many people celebrate Christmas as a secular holiday rather than in its religious tradition. What kinds of things and traditions do we associate with the secular celebration? [snowmen, Rudolph the Red-Nosed Reindeer, Frosty the Snowman, gift-giving, lots of shopping, "winter" songs like I'll Be Home For Christmas, etc.]
- Does anyone have family Christmas traditions you'd like to share with the class? If you celebrate Christmas either in a religious or secular way, what does your family do every Christmas? [Answers will vary.]

Activity #3
Share with students the writing assignment "My Perfect Christmas." Another holiday can be substituted if preferred for this writing assignment. Discuss the writing assignment directions in detail, give students ample time to complete the assignment, and tell students when the assignment will be collected for grading.

STUDY QUESTIONS ANSWER KEY
Dear Mr. Henshaw Reading Assignment 4

December 22 - December 25

1. What are some of the ways that Leigh tries to keep people from stealing his lunch?

   Leigh tries to keep people from stealing his lunch by eating it on the way to school and watching who goes behind the partition where the lunches are kept. After Christmas he plans to put a fictitious name on his bag.

2. Since Leigh's dad did not spend Christmas with them the first year after the divorce, how does Leigh get his present?

   Leigh's dad's Christmas present is delivered to their house by a trucker who responds to his dad's radio request for help in delivering the package.

WRITING ASSIGNMENT: MY PERFECT CHRISTMAS
Dear Mr. Henshaw

Prompt

"[The quilted down jacket] was the right size and felt great. Getting a present from my Dad in time for Christmas felt even better." –Leigh Botts

Getting that jacket from his dad made Leigh's whole Christmas. It was a gift he wanted, but most importantly, his dad remembered to give him *something*, and it arrived before Christmas morning.

We've talked about Leigh's Christmas--and Christmas traditions in general, in both religious and secular contexts. Imagine what your perfect Christmas Day would be like. If you don't celebrate Christmas, you can substitute your favorite other holiday. What would make that day special for you personally? Having family together? Getting or giving a particular present? Feasting? Having a particular role in a play or pageant? Limitless decorating with lights, music, and all the bells and whistles? Baking & decorating racks and racks of cookies?

Assignment

Write a descriptive essay in which you tell all about your perfect Christmas (or other holiday) Day.

Ways To Begin (Pre-writing)

- Take a few minutes and daydream about your special day. Let your imagination go, and consider even impossible possibilities. What would be The Best Day Ever? Make a list of everything that comes to mind.

- Look at your list and circle the best things. Narrow your list some more by deciding which of the things you've circled could actually be done in one full day? Now you have the Best Of The Best! Scratch out the others.

- Next, organize the Best Of The Best in an order that would be likely for them to take place. Number them then rewrite them in order with several lines of space in between them.

- Consider each of the items separately. Under each one jot down things you want to remember to say about each--details, descriptions, phrases. Be creative and specific. Use sensory words and some similes (comparing using "like" or "as").

Dear Mr. Henshaw Writing Assignment "My Perfect Christmas" Page 2

Begin Writing (Drafting)
- Write out the paragraphs for each item on your list using the details you have jotted down. Don't panic if you can't get them all in or if you come up with others that are better. *Drafting* means you play around with the ideas you have to make it the best it can be. Writing is more of an art than an exact science.

- Transition from one paragraph to another. This is your chance to cleverly slip from one idea to the next without over-using "and then" or "next." Some alternatives could be:
    - I couldn't believe it when…
    - The high (or low) point of the day would be…
    - Just when I thought things couldn't get worse (or better)…
    - But the thing that would mean the most to me would be…

    _____
    _____
    _____

- Add a few more examples to the list above to get the knack of writing transitions.

- Remember to add an introduction and a conclusion–a paragraph or so at the beginning and a paragraph or so at the end. If you have trouble with these, don't sit there stuck and unhappy; ask for help. All writers–even the most famous ones--need someone to bounce ideas off of and to give them some objective pointers.

- Erase, scratch, edit, rearrange, substitute…work with your words until you are happy with them. You may end up with a whole bunch of different drafts as you work your way to your masterpiece.

Proofreading
When you are satisfied with your work, write it out neatly and look it over for typos, grammatical errors, & things that seem unclear or out of order. Fix those things.

Final Draft
Then give your work to someone else (whose opinion you trust to be helpful) to read. Consider his/her suggestions, make the corrections you need to make, and create a final copy.

LESSON TWELVE
Dear Mr. Henshaw

Objectives
1. Students will preview the study questions for Reading Assignment 5.
2. Students will read Reading Assignment 5.
3. Students will discuss the study questions for Reading Assignment 5.
4. Students will learn about pseudonyms, Hermiston Oregon, the Columbia River, and juke boxes.
5. Students will learn about figurative language--specifically, hyperboles.
6. Students will study Mr. Findley's character in more detail.
7. Students will explore the idea of listening and writing dialogue.

Activity #1
Have students preview the study questions for Reading Assignment 5 (in whatever way you choose).

Activity #2
If you have not yet completed the oral reading evaluations or if you wish to continue with another round of them, have students read Assignment 5 orally. Otherwise, students may read silently or in pairs.

Activity #3
After students have read Assignment 5, answer the study questions together as a whole class.

Activity #4
Do any or all of the Additional Points For Discussion & Activities for Reading Assignment 5.

STUDY QUESTIONS
Dear Mr. Henshaw Reading Assignment 5

Section Five: Pages 45-53

1. Who is Joe Kelly?

2. Leigh writes more about Mr. Fridley in the entries for January 8 and 9. What does Mr. Fridley do as he stands by the garbage can at lunch time?

3. Who comes up with the idea of putting a burglar alarm on Leigh's lunch bag?

4. Why does Leigh ask his mom why she doesn't get married again?

STUDY QUESTIONS ANSWER KEY
Dear Mr. Henshaw Reading Assignment 5

Section Five: Pages 45-53

1. Who is Joe Kelly?

   Joe Kelly is the name of the boy in Ways to Amuse a Dog. Leigh takes this name as a pseudonym to write on his lunch bag to fool the lunch thief.

2. Leigh writes more about Mr. Fridley in the entries for January 8 and 9. What does Mr. Fridley do as he stands by the garbage can at lunch time?

   Mr. Fridley makes sure kids don't throw away their flatware or their retainers. He talks and jokes with the kids.

3. Who comes up with the idea of putting a burglar alarm on Leigh's lunch bag?

   Mr. Fridley comes up with the idea. He is just joking with Leigh, but Leigh thinks it's a good idea.

4. Why does Leigh ask his mom why she doesn't get married again?

   Leigh thinks that if he had a father handy, his father could help him put a burglar alarm onto his lunch bag.

ADDITIONAL POINTS FOR DISCUSSION & ACTIVITIES
Dear Mr. Henshaw, Reading Assignment 5

Pseudonyms: In his January 3 entry, Leigh writes, "Today I wrote a fictitious name, or pseud. as they sometimes say, on my lunchbag."

- Ask students if they know what "pseud." is an abbreviation for. Let them guess if they don't know. Explain what a pseudonym is and give some examples of people who have used pseudonyms in the past. (Mark Twain for Samuel Clemens is one they might be familiar with.)

- Ask students if they know what an "alias" is. [It is a false name used to hide one's true identity.] Discuss how *alias* is different from *pseudonym*. You might say that a pseudonym is a specific kind of an alias, and you might note that sometimes *alias* has a negative connotation in the sense that criminals sometimes use aliases to conceal their true identities to hide from the law.

- In a way, our screen names on chat and other places are aliases. Discuss how those are used for our own protection instead of for criminal activities.

- Activity: Ask students to choose a pseudonym–a pen name–and to explain why they would choose that name.

Internet Excursion: Take a class excursion on the Internet to find out about Hermiston, Oregon, the Columbia River, and juke boxes.

Idiom & Hyperbole: Mr. Fridley tells Leigh, "Cheer up, Leigh, or you'll trip over your lower lip." This little phrase is an example of an idiom as well as hyperbole. Ask students if they know what this phrase means and can guess why we use it. [When we pout, our lower lip often sticks out. The more we pout, the more it sticks out. Someone (like Leigh) who is really down in the dumps (another idiom!) might have their lower lip poked way out.

Could Leigh actually trip over his lower lip? Of course not. It is an exaggeration, which is what hyperbole is–a kind of figure of speech that shows exaggeration. Here are a few other examples of hyperbole:
>I'm so hungry I could eat a horse.
>If I don't get to go to the dance, I'll just die!
>Rick hit the baseball into the next state!

Have students think of more examples.

Dear Mr. Henshaw Additional Points For Discussion & Activities, Reading Assignment 5

Character Study, Mr. Fridley: Ask students, "What have we seen Mr. Fridley do so far in the book?" [He let Leigh help with the flags, reminded kids not to throw away their flatware or retainers, and gave Leigh the idea about putting a burglar alarm on his lunchbag.] Put students into small groups to complete the Character Fact graphic organizer that follows this lesson. Distribute copies, discuss the directions, and give students ample time to complete the task. When students have completed the task, come back together as a class to discuss the answers.

Listening & Writing Dialogue: In the entry of January 10, Leigh writes, "I guess you meant to listen and write down the way people talk, sort of like a play."

- Ask students to think of someone they could pretend to be for a few minutes. They could choose a character from television or the movies, a person from history, a famous politician, a rapper, a sports figure, a relative, a friend, a teacher...anyone. Students could get together and work in pairs if their characters "go together" (like Laurel & Hardy or two characters from the same television show). Tell students to take a few minutes to think who they want to portray, to think of what the person would say or do, and to think about how the person would talk or act. After students have had a few minutes to prepare, let each student take a few seconds to do the impersonation.

- Briefly examine the impersonations with your students to point out differences in the way each character spoke. Also point out that this is what Mr. Henshaw wants Leigh to listen for, to help him when he writes *dialogue*.

- Discuss with students the differences between writing a narrative (which is what most of Leigh's entries are) as opposed to writing dialogue (which is what he uses in the last part of the January 10th entry). Make a list of all the things your students can think of that differentiate the two forms, including (but not limited to) the format on the page and the effect of the formats. Which is a more powerful presentation? Which gives you more information? Which is easier to develop a mental picture from? Answers will vary; the point is to get students thinking about the effects of the form of the materials they read.

- Follow-Up: Have students choose another entry from *Dear Mr. Henshaw* to write in a play format.

CHARACTER FACTS
Dear Mr. Henshaw: Mr. Fridley

Start at the beginning of the book and skim read to find examples of things Mr. Fridley does and things Leigh says about Mr. Fridley. Write them down in the correct columns, then in the right column, state what we learn about Mr. Fridley from each action or statement. Use the back of the page to continue if you find more examples than there are rows in the chart.

WHAT MR. FRIDLEY DOES	WHAT LEIGH SAYS ABOUT MR. FRIDLEY	WHAT WE LEARN ABOUT MR. FRIDLEY

CHARACTER FACTS SUGGESTED ANSWERS
Dear Mr. Henshaw: Mr. Fridley

There are many examples students could choose. Here are a few:

WHAT MR. FRIDLEY DOES	WHAT LEIGH SAYS ABOUT MR. FRIDLEY	WHAT WE LEARN ABOUT MR. FRIDLEY
	"He's always fair about who gets to pass out milk at lunchtime, and once when he had to clean up after someone who threw up in the hall, he didn't even look cross."	Mr. Fridley is fair. He is compassionate, understanding that the person who threw up already felt bad and didn't need scolding.
Mr. Fridley invites Leigh to come help with the flags in the morning.		Mr. Fridley knows Leigh is a new boy at school and tries to make him feel a part of things. This again shows Mr. Fridley's compassion and interest in others.
	"Mr. Fridley is so funny."	Mr. Fridley has a good sense of humor. It could also mean "funny" in the sense of having unexpected behavior, different from parents or teachers.
Mr. Fridley stands by the garbage can at lunch to remind students not to throw away their flatware or retainers.		It's probably his job to watch out for the flatware so the school doesn't have to buy more, but he also looks out for things the kids shouldn't throw away. Again, he shows an interest in the kids and their well-being.
Mr Fridley says, "Look out! Don't lose your false teeth."		Mr. Fridley has a sense of humor.
Mr. Fridley suggests a burglar alarm for Leigh's lunchbag.		Mr. Fridley thinks of funny things. He has a good sense of humor and a creative mind.
Mr. Fridley says, "Cheer up Leigh, or you'll trip over your lower lip."		Mr. Fridley doesn't like to see Leigh upset, and he exaggerates and makes a joke to try to cheer him up. Mr. Fridley cares about Leigh.

LESSON THIRTEEN
Dear Mr. Henshaw

Objectives
1. Students will learn about the vocabulary words for Reading Assignment 6: *decided, hibernated, mimeograph,* and *nuisance.*
2. Students will preview the study questions for Reading Assignment 6.
3. Students will read Reading Assignment 6.
4. Students will locate Yellowstone Park, Kansas, and Wyoming on a map and learn a little bit about Yellowstone.

Activity #1
Preview the vocabulary words for Reading Assignment 6 with students. The vocabulary pages following this daily lesson are meant for use with a whiteboard, but you may make copies for your student if you wish.

Activity #2
Preview the study questions for Reading Assignment 6 with your students. Read through them and see what predictions students can make about what will happen in this section of the book.

Activity #3
Have students read Reading Assignment 6 in whatever way you think is appropriate (oral reading, silent reading, partners, etc.) This is a short reading assignment which students should be able to finish in class with a little time left over.

Activity #4
Have students locate Yellowstone National Park, Kansas, and Wyoming on a map of the U.S. Then go online to view a short video about Yellowstone. YouTube has several very short ones (5 minutes) that give students a flavor for the area. Some feature bears, which are the subject of Mr. Henshaw's newest book.

Dear Mr. Henshaw
Vocabulary For Reading Assignment 6

NUISANCE (repeat from Assignment 3)
"I know you're busy and I don't want to be a nuisance." (Page 59)

Do you remember what nuisance means?
What is its definition?

_____

Which would be more of a nuisance: a wad of gum stuck to your shoe or your little brother wanting you to play with him while you're doing your homework? Justify your answer.

What's the difference between *nuisance* and *pest*? What are the connotations and denotations of these words?

Dear Mr. Henshaw
Vocabulary For Reading Assignment 6

MIMEOGRAPH

"She said our school along with some other schools is going to print (that means mimeograph) a book of work of young authors...." (Page 58)

Before copy machines and digital printers were invented, people sometimes **mimeographed** to make paper copies. A person typed on a typewriter (usually on a setting that did not use the ink ribbon) onto a special paper called stencil paper. The action of the keys literally cut the stencil paper, making a master.

Then, the person would take the stencil and secure it around the "drum" of a **mimeograph** machine and load the machine with ink and blank paper. When the person turned the handle of the machine, the stencil on the drum would roll around, the machine would feed a blank sheet of paper, and the ink would go through the stencil to print the words on the page. The ink dried pretty fast, so one could crank the handle and make copies at a pretty good speed.

Look at the parts of the word: mimeograph
What does mime mean? What does graph mean?

Put them together, and you have the function of this machine!

Dear Mr. Henshaw
Vocabulary For Reading Assignment 6

HIBERNATED

"When they **hibernated** and then woke up in the middle of winter because they had eaten all the wrong things and hadn't stored up enough fat, I almost cried." (Page 56-57)

What does **hibernated** mean?

took a nap   became seasonally inactive   slept

Which animals **hibernate**?

deer   dogs   frogs   bears   moose   box turtles   elephants

When animals go into a state of **hibernation**, their body temperature usually drops, their breathing and heart rate slow down, and their metabolic rate slows down.

Is **hibernating** something you think you would like to do? Why?

Make a sentence using the word **hibernated**.

_____

Dear Mr. Henshaw
Vocabulary For Reading Assignment 6

DECIDED

"...then I got to thinking (you said authors should think) and **decided** a book doesn't have to be funny to be good...." (Page 56)

You probably already know what **decided** means. Write a definition here:

_____

The word decided is included in your vocabulary work for the spelling. Sometimes it's hard to remember the correct spelling when a "c" sounds like an "s" and an "e" sounds a little like an "i."

When you come upon words like this, sometimes there's no good way to remember the spelling but to memorize it; then you have it in your personal word bank for life. :-)

Write the word **decided** 10 times and say the letters out loud as you write them. Saying it, hearing it, and writing it are good memorization aids. To practice spelling this word, at home, dance around your bedroom spelling **decided** in a rhythm, like a cheerleader's cheer.

STUDY QUESTIONS
Dear Mr. Henshaw Reading Assignment 6

Reading Assignment 6 (January 12 - January 19)

1. The librarian stops Leigh in the hall and asks him to come to the library. Why?

2. What does Leigh worry about some nights while he lies awake listening to the gas station pinging?

3. Why does Leigh think his dad isn't very interested in him?

4. According to Leigh's teacher, his writing skills are improving. Why do you think that is?

5. How could Leigh win lunch with a Famous Author?

LESSON FOURTEEN
Dear Mr. Henshaw

Objectives
1. Students will discuss and answer the study questions for Reading Assignment 6.
2. Students will study a specific instance of inference in this assignment.
3. Students will discuss how Mr. Henshaw's bear story relates to Leigh's life.
4. Students will discuss the importance of doing what you say you will do.
5. Students will learn about the Newbery Award and other book awards.

Activity #1
Give students some time to develop answers to the study questions for Reading Assignment 6 (individually, in pairs, in groups, or as a whole class). Then, take time to briefly discuss the answers (unless you already have done so as a whole class).

Activity #2
Do any or all of the Additional Points For Discussion & Activities for Reading Assignment 6.

STUDY QUESTIONS ANSWER KEY
Dear Mr. Henshaw Reading Assignment 6

Reading Assignment 6 (January 12 - January 19)

1. The librarian stops Leigh in the hall and asks him to come to the library. Why?

    The librarian has Mr. Henshaw's new book and tells Leigh he can be the first one to read it. She says that she knows he loves books by Mr. Henshaw because he checks them out so often.

2. What does Leigh worry about some nights while he lies awake listening to the gas station pinging?

    He worries that something might happen to his mother.

3. Why does Leigh think his dad isn't very interested in him?

    Leigh's dad doesn't call when he says he will.

4. According to Leigh's teacher, his writing skills are improving. Why do you think that is?

    Leigh's writing skills are improving because he is doing what Mr. Henshaw told him to do. He is reading and writing a lot.

5. How could Leigh win lunch with a Famous Author?

    If the story he submits for the book of work of young authors is one of the best pieces submitted, he and a few others winners will get to go to lunch with a Famous Author.

ADDITIONAL POINTS FOR DISCUSSION & ACTIVITIES
Dear Mr. Henshaw, Reading Assignment 6

Inferences: "[The librarian] said she knew how much I love your books since I check them out so often. Now I know Mr. Fridley isn't the only one who notices me." –Leigh Botts, January 12.

1. How does Leigh know that Mr. Fridley isn't the only one who notices him?
    The librarian pays enough attention to know what books he likes and goes to the trouble of saving one for him.

2. What could you infer about the librarian from her actions?
    – The librarian *does* notice Leigh and tries to do something nice for him.
    – She may be good at her job, since she found Leigh an appropriate book.
    – Like Mr. Fridley, she may be reaching out to Leigh to make him feel at home in his new school.
    – If that is the case, she is probably a compassionate person.

Leigh and The Bear Story
Reading a story can sometimes make us think about our own lives. We can relate to a character or a situation, and we think about that after we close the book. This is one of the benefits of reading...it prompts us to think about situations and our own lives.

What two things does Leigh say in his January 15th entry that relates Mr. Henshaw's bear story to Leigh's own life?
    "I wonder what happens to the fathers of bears. Do they just go away?"
        Leigh has been thinking about the orphaned bear cubs and wonders about their dad, perhaps because he can relate to them, not having a dad at home either.
    "... I worry because something might happen to Mom."
        Leigh sees that the orphaned cubs could easily have perished without their mother if they hadn't been saved, and he may wonder what would happen to himself if something happened to his own mother.

So, in what ways is Leigh like the bear cubs?
    Like the cubs, he doesn't have a father at home. Also, he is vulnerable until he becomes full-grown and independent.

Dear Mr. Henshaw ADDITIONAL POINTS FOR DISCUSSION & ACTIVITIES Reading Assignment 6 Page 2

Relationships

"I don't think Dad is that much interested in me. He didn't phone when he said he would."
–Leigh Botts, January 15

1. Does not phoning when you say you will mean that you are not interested in the person you said you would call?
There are a few important points to bring out in this discussion:
- Not phoning doesn't necessarily mean you are not interested in the person, but it could mean that.
- The frequency of not calling when you say you will makes a difference. One instance is different from a pattern of not calling.
- Consider the point of view. To Leigh, the call is the most important thing in the world whereas Leigh's dad has many concerns with his job and his own life.
- Leigh doesn't consider all the reasons that may have kept his dad from calling. What could some of those reasons be?

2. What can we infer about Leigh's dad from this quote?
- We could think that he's a jerk for not calling his son, or we could take an understanding point of view and empathize with him that life gets busy and it's easy to forget to do something we say we will. How many in your class empathize with Leigh's dad? It should be an interesting discussion.
- You can take this opportunity to talk about how we need to be careful about judging others when we don't know the exact circumstances of their actions.

3. So what can we learn from this little quote from the book?
- We need to be careful in our own relationships to do what we say we will do because it can make a big difference to some people and in some circumstances.
- We need to be careful about judging others until we know their own circumstances.
- What means everything in the world to one person may be just another thing in a long list for someone else.
- We should consider others' points of view, not just our own.

Book Awards

"I hope your book wins a million awards." – Leigh Botts, January 15
Go on line and explore with your students the many different kinds of book awards that are given. See which of the awarded titles your students have read. Some popular awards are:
    The Pulitzer Prize
    The Newbery Medal (which Beverly Cleary won for *Dear. Mr. Henshaw*)
    The Coretta Scott King Award
    The National Book Award

LESSON FIFTEEN
Dear Mr. Henshaw

Objectives
1. Students will review information covered in reading assignments 3-6.
2. Students will preview the vocabulary words for Reading Assignment 7.
3. Students will preview the study questions for Reading Assignment 7.
4. Students will read Reading Assignment 7.

Activity #1
Use the review page that follows this lesson to review some vocabulary and events from Reading Assignments 3-6. Do it together as a class using your whiteboard, or make copies for individuals or pairs to complete. Briefly discuss the answers.

Activity #2
Preview the vocabulary words for Reading Assignment 7. The vocabulary pages that follow this lesson are meant for use with a whiteboard as a whole-class discussion, but you may make copies for students in your class if you prefer that.

Activity #3
Have students take a few minutes to look over the study questions to become familiar with key words and ideas in Reading Assignment 7.

Activity #4
Have students read Reading Assignment 7 silently for the remainder of this class period. This reading should be completed prior to the next class meeting.

REVIEW: READING ASSIGNMENTS 3-6
Dear Mr. Henshaw

Using the words below, fill in the blanks.

RUDE   FLAG   PSEUDONYM   CUBS   SIMILE   SHOE

LUNCH   FICTITIOUS   DIORAMA   FICTION   TRUCKER   ALARM

1. Leigh's problem is that people keep stealing the good things out of his _____.

2. Mr. Fridley thinks Leigh should come early to help raise the _____.

3. A divorced person is like a lost _____.

4. #3 is an example of a _____.

5. After Christmas Leigh plans to put a _____ name on his bag.

6. Leigh's dad's Christmas present is delivered to their house by a _____.

7. Leigh is like the _____: no father at home and vulnerable.

8. Dear Mr. Henshaw is an example of _____.

9. It would be _____ to slam a door in someone's face.

10. We enjoyed looking at the _____ of the battlefield.

11. Joe Kelly is the _____ Leigh puts on his lunch bag.

12. Mr Fridley comes up with the idea for putting an _____ on the lunch bag.

REVIEW ANSWER KEY: READING ASSIGNMENTS 3-6
Dear Mr. Henshaw

Using the words below, fill in the blanks.

| RUDE | FLAG | PSEUDONYM | CUBS | SIMILE | SHOE |
| LUNCH | FICTITIOUS | DIORAMA | FICTION | TRUCKER | ALARM |

1. Leigh's problem is that people keep stealing the good things out of his LUNCH.

2. Mr. Fridley thinks Leigh should come early to help raise the FLAG.

3. A divorced person is like a lost SHOE.

4. #3 is an example of a SIMILE.

5. After Christmas Leigh plans to put a FICTITIOUS name on his bag.

6. Leigh's dad's Christmas present is delivered to their house by a TRUCKER.

7. Leigh is like the CUBS: no father at home and vulnerable.

8. Dear Mr. Henshaw is an example of FICTION.

9. It would be RUDE to slam a door in someone's face.

10. We enjoyed looking at the DIORAMA of the battlefield.

11. Joe Kelly is the PSEUDONYM Leigh puts on his lunch bag.

12. Mr. Fridley comes up with the idea for putting an ALARM on the lunch bag.

Dear Mr. Henshaw
Vocabulary For Reading Assignment 7

SCOWLING

Mr. Fridley noticed me scowling again and said, "So the lunchbag thief strikes again!" (Page 62)

Consider the context above and circle the word that is something scowling might mean.

smiling   pushing   sweating   frowning   eating

People frown when they are unhappy, sad, angry, or uncertain. Some people have a frown on their faces naturally–they're not necessarily feeling any of the aforementioned emotions.

Scowling is frowning, but it has connotation of frowning because you are angry or upset.

What might cause you to scowl?

_____

Use any form of the word scowling in a sentence.

_____

Dear Mr. Henshaw
Vocabulary For Reading Assignment 7

COMFORTABLE

"I wish I had a grandfather like Mr. Fridley. He is so nice, sort of baggy and comfortable." (Page 62)

Most of you probably already know what comfortable means. You have a comfortable pair of jeans or a comfortable shirt. Perhaps an air-conditioned room is comfortable on a hot, summer day.

If something or someone comforts you, the thing or the person makes you feel better, feel at ease.

In the passage above, Leigh describes Mr. Fridley as "baggy and comfortable." What does comfortable mean in this case?

_____
_____
_____

Write some other words that come to your mind to describe Mr. Fridley when you hear him described as "baggy and comfortable."

Dear Mr. Henshaw
Vocabulary For Reading Assignment 7

ULCERS

"Sometimes they get ulcers from the strain of trying to make good time on the highway." (Page 63)

It's hard to tell what ulcers are from the context of this sentence. Do you think they're a good thing or a bad thing? Why?

Did you ever get a stomach ache when you were nervous about something? When we get nervous or stressed, sometimes our stomachs make too much digestive fluid (sometimes called stomach acid). When that happens over a long period of time, it can cause ulcers in the stomach.

Ulcers are damaged areas where the stomach lining starts to break down. They can be painful, and left untreated they can be dangerous to your health. There are other kinds of ulcers, too. You can get ulcers in your mouth or on your skin, caused by things other than stomach acid.

Use the word ulcers in a sentence of your own.

_____

Dear Mr. Henshaw
Vocabulary For Reading Assignment 7

DESERT

"He loves the mountains and the desert sunrises..." (Page 63)

Again, you probably already know what a desert is—that dry place where not much grows but scrubby plants and cacti.

The reason you have this vocabulary word is for the spelling. It is often confused with dessert (the delicious sweet stuff you eat after dinner). Desert (the dry place) has one "s," and dessert (the sweet stuff) has two "s"es.

One way to remember the spelling is to think, "I always want more dessert...there are more 's'es in dessert." More dessert, more "s"es.

Can you think of another way to remember
the spelling difference?

_____

Use desert in a sentence.

_____

Dear Mr. Henshaw
Vocabulary For Reading Assignment 7

WRATH

"I am filled with wrath .... I am mad at Mom for divorcing Dad." (Page 64)

What do you think wrath means?

anger   happiness   sadness   envy

What other word in the sentence gives you a clue about the meaning of wrath?

Wrath is actually more than anger. It's a resentful anger, an anger that makes you feel like you want to lash out or punish someone. It is strong and deep.

What effect has the divorce had on Leigh, and why would that make him filled with wrath?

Dear Mr. Henshaw
Vocabulary For Reading Assignment 7

MILDEW

"I was supposed to scrub off some of the mildew on the bathroom walls with some smelly stuff, but I didn't...." (Page 68)

What is mildew?
fungus   soap scum   water stains

Bleach is the best mildew remover, but bleach is dangerous stuff. If it spills onto your skin, it can cause ulcers. If you get it in your eyes, it can make you blind. If you swallow it, it can kill you. It's nasty, nasty stuff—but it kills mildew! Most people dilute bleach in water or use some other kind of smelly bathroom cleaner (like the one Leigh was supposed to use) because it's safer.

Mildew comes in different colors, but it's usually a whitish color. It's a fungus that grows in damp, warm conditions like Leigh's bathroom. It's kind of like mold.

How can you prevent mildew from forming so you don't have to clean it up with smelly, nasty chemicals?

Did you know plants can get mildew, too?

Dear Mr. Henshaw
Vocabulary For Reading Assignment 7

RECEIVER

"I picked up the receiver and dialed Dad's number over in Bakersfield." (Page 68)

A **receiver** is someone or something that receives (gets) something. How many kinds of "receivers" can you think of?

When phones were first invented, they looked like this:

Receiver ➡ The thing you picked up to listen to the caller was called the receiver; you received the voice. There was no number pad or dial because you just picked up and told the operator who you wanted to call. The thing that looks like the phone's eyes is the bell ringer, and the thing that looks like the phone's nose is the part you talked into.

Leigh's phone probably looked like this: Receiver

The receiver and the part where you spoke into were combined into the "receiver." The dial had numbers 0-9 and you could dial a person's number directly without an operator.

Compare and contrast our phones today with these.

Dear Mr. Henshaw
Vocabulary For Reading Assignment 7

RECEPTION

"Mountains cut down on reception," Dad told me. (Page 72)

Reception is on your vocabulary list for this section of the book for the spelling, not for the meaning. Most of you probably know about cell phone reception, that how well the call you are receiving comes through often depends on where you are. You get better reception when you are near or have an unobstructed line to the signal.

Spelling reception is a little different. The "c" sounds like an "s" and the "tion" sounds like "shun."

Write 3 different sentences using the word reception, to practice the usage and spelling.

_____

_____

_____

STUDY QUESTIONS
Dear Mr. Henshaw Reading Assignment 7

Reading Assignment 7 (January 20 - February 4)

1. How does Leigh feel when his father doesn't call?

2. What happens to Bandit while he is traveling with Leigh's father in the rig?

3. According to Leigh's mom, a trucker's life is not easy. Why?

4. Why is Leigh upset about the sugar refinery shutting down near his home?

5. What does Leigh's mom think are the reasons that Leigh's dad loves trucking?

LESSON SIXTEEN
Dear Mr. Henshaw

Objectives
1. Students will discuss the Study Questions for Reading Assignment 7.
2. Students will work in small groups to determine the main events and ideas for Reading Assignment 7.
3. Students will write a narrative summarizing the important events and ideas for Reading Assignment 7.

Activity #1
Discuss the answers to the Study Questions for Reading Assignment 7 as a whole class.

Activity #2
Direct students into small groups. Each group should discuss the events within Reading Assignment 7 to determine which things are important enough to include in a summary of this section of the book. Each student in the group should write down (in order) the main events the group decides are noteworthy.

Activity #3
Distribute the Narrative Writing Assignment and discuss the directions in detail. Students should use the remainder of this class time to work on this assignment. Tell students when their work will be due.

STUDY QUESTIONS ANSWER KEY
Dear Mr. Henshaw Reading Assignment 7

Reading Assignment 7 (January 20 - February 4)

1. How does Leigh feel when his father doesn't call?
    Leigh feels sad, lonely, hurt, and disappointed.

2. What happens to Bandit while he is traveling with Leigh's father in the rig?
    Bandit jumps out of the truck in a snow storm and does not come back to the truck. The road is about to close, and Leigh's father has to leave, so Bandit is left behind.

3. According to Leigh's mom, a trucker's life is not easy. Why?
    Truckers sometimes lose some of their hearing in their left ear from the wind rushing past the driver's window. Truckers also get out of shape from sitting such long hours without exercise and from eating too much greasy food. Sometimes they get ulcers from the strain of trying to make good time on the highway.

4. Why is Leigh upset about the sugar refinery shutting down near his home?
    Leigh is afraid he will never see his father again if the refinery shuts down giving his father no work-related reason to come to the area.

5. What does Leigh's mom think are the reasons that Leigh's dad loves trucking?
    Leigh's mom thinks Leigh's dad loves trucking because he loves the feel of power when he is sitting high in his cab controlling a mighty machine. He loves the excitement of never knowing where his next trip will take him. He loves the mountains and the desert sunrises and the sight of the orange trees heavy with oranges and the smell of fresh-mown alfalfa.

NARRATIVE WRITING ASSIGNMENT
Dear Mr. Henshaw

Prompt

Re-telling important information is something everyone needs to know how to do. The first step in relaying information is to know what is important enough to pass along.

We make decisions all the time about which parts of a story are important enough to pass along, depending on the situation. Consider what you think about when someone asks you, "What did you do at school today." You decide which things to tell and which things not to tell.

This is what you have just completed in your group work. You decided which things in Reading Assignment 7 were important enough to include in a summary of this section of the book.

Assignment

Your assignment is to write a narrative summary of Reading Assignment 7. Here's the "tricky" part of the assignment: don't use "next," "then," "and then," or "after that." Relay the story using other ways to connect the events and ideas. Use at least one direct quote from a character in the story.

Drafting

The pre-writing is already done: you have a list of things to include in your narrative. Review the list. Pretend you've been telling your friend about the book as you have been reading it. Now your friend has asked you, "So, what happens in this section of the book?". What would you say? Start writing.

When you have finished your rough draft, go back and edit it. Rewrite awkward places, remove and rewrite places where you used the "forbidden" connecting words or phrases, and check your organization, sentence lengths, and grammar. Make it your best work.

Proofreading & Editing

When you are satisfied with your narrative, have someone else read it—someone you trust to give you thoughtful, constructive criticism and good suggestions. Consider that person's comments, decide which comments would improve your work, and edit your work accordingly.

Final Draft

Do a final proofreading and make a final draft of your narrative.

LESSON SEVENTEEN
Dear Mr. Henshaw

Objectives
1. Students will read Reading Assignment 8.
2. Students will discuss the importance of Reading Assignment 8 in the context of the novel.
3. Students will discuss the development and growth of Leigh through this point in the book.

Activity #1
This is a short but important reading assignment. There aren't a lot of study questions, but we can really start to see some growth and development in the character of Leigh. Tell students to look for clues about Leigh's growth as a character and person as they read this section of the book.

Have students read the February 5th entry. They should be able to finish this during class time.

Activity #2
Discuss the two Study Guide questions for Reading Assignment 8 as a whole class. Explain that this chapter is a turning point in the novel, as Leigh discovers and learns to forgive his father's shortcomings.

Activity #3
Spend time looking at Leigh as a character/person. Write notes as the discussion progresses for students to copy for study purposes. Here are some questions to help you guide a class discussion. Some of this may be a little above your students' level, but use what you can and use your usual style of communicating ideas with your students. The answers/notes are really more for you than as a "lecture" for students.

1. Leigh says, "Yesterday after I hung up on Dad I flopped down on my bed and cried and swore and pounded my pillow." Why did Leigh do that?

To this point in the story, Leigh has been seeing his dad as *his* dad–belonging to him and his mom, even though they are a divorced family. He dreams and wishes that his dad would take him to school on his big rig. He remembers times when he has traveled with his dad and things they used to do together. He waits by the phone for his dad to call. When it becomes clear to Leigh that his dad belongs to someone else now, everything changes. Someone else is more important to his dad than Leigh is, which explains why his dad doesn't call.

This realization is a growing-up moment for Leigh. He has no choice but to accept that his dad is gone, the divorce is real. He knows "he wouldn't have phoned me at all, no matter what he said." Leigh cries from hurt and loss. He pounds his pillow and swears out of anger caused by the hurt he feels.

The lesson he is learning is that life goes on. No matter what happens or how much we want to hang on to the past, life goes on. We can either deal with it and accept it and move on, too, or be mired in misery wishing things would always be the same.

2. In the February 4th entry, Leigh says, "*I hate my father.*" Yet, in this entry (February 5th) he says, "And I don't hate my father. I can't hate him. Maybe things would be easier if I could."

Point out that each entry is written after the day's events have taken place. So when Leigh is writing the February 4th entry, he has just found out about his dad's other family. When he writes the February 5th entry, he has already had the conversations with his mother. This is an important fact to establish–the time sequence of when events happen versus when Leigh writes about them.

How does this change in Leigh's attitude show he is growing up?

Leigh recognizes that his father has faults. [What faults does Leigh recognize his father has?]
- He knows his father doesn't always call when he says he will.
- He knows his father doesn't always exactly tell him the truth. (His dad tells him, "I could've sworn I [left the door open for Bandit]" and Leigh knows that because his father says it this way, he probably didn't leave the door open at all.)

Yet, even though Leigh recognizes his father's faults, he no longer hates his father. Why not?
- He got a lot of anger towards his father out of his system by swearing and pounding his pillow and crying the night before.
- He recognizes now that life moves on.
- In the conversation with his mom, Leigh begins to understand that his father is somewhat irresponsible; he's not very grown-up.
- Leigh's mom doesn't seem to hate his father. She seems to have reconciled herself to the fact that his dad has faults but also has good points. When she says, "Your Dad has many good qualities," it causes Leigh to consider that possibility. Leigh's mom's attitude towards his dad goes a long way towards forming Leigh's attitude.

Being able to recognize a person's faults–and to forgive them for perceived wrongdoings because you understand those inherent faults–is a sign of maturity. Being able to look more objectively at a situation--in this case Leigh's seeing his dad as a person through his mom's conversation–is an adult ability. A child only sees "this hurts me" and cries or gets mad. An adult says, "This hurts me, but now I understand why it does, and I can accept that reason as a way to live with the situation." It's a more rational, reasoning way to handle a problem.

Why might things be easier if Leigh could hate his father?

If he could hate his father, Leigh could just write him off and not think about him anymore. Since he still cares for his father, Leigh is still subject to feeling hurt and disappointed when his father doesn't live up to Leigh's expectations.

STUDY QUESTIONS
Dear Mr. Henshaw Reading Assignment 8

Reading Assignment 8 (February 5)

1. What does Leigh's mom mean when she says Leigh's dad will never grow up?

2. Leigh's mom used to ride with his dad in the truck on trips, but she says that she got tired of doing that. Why does that make Leigh feel better?

STUDY QUESTIONS ANSWER KEY
Dear Mr. Henshaw Reading Assignment 8

Reading Assignment 8 (February 5)
1. What does Leigh's mom mean when she says Leigh's dad will never grow up?
    She means that Leigh's father will never change. He will never learn to take responsibility for anything other than his truck.

2. Leigh's mom used to ride with his dad in the truck on trips, but she says that she got tired of doing that. Why does that make Leigh feel better?
    It makes Leigh feel better because it means that she did not give up riding with his dad because he was born, but rather because she simply didn't like doing it anymore and wanted to stop.

LESSON EIGHTEEN
Dear Mr. Henshaw

Objectives
1. Students will preview the vocabulary words for Reading Assignment 9: *antique, molest, quivering*, and *weird*.
2. Students will preview the study questions for Reading Assignment 9.
3. Students will read Reading Assignment 9.
4. Students will view a short video about Monarch butterflies and write a descriptive paragraph

Activity #1
Preview the vocabulary words for Reading Assignment 9 with your students using the pages that follow this lesson. These pages are meant for use with a whiteboard, but you may copy them for your students if you prefer that.

After previewing the vocabulary words, ask students what they know happens in this reading assignment, based on the quotes from the text in which the vocabulary words appear.

Activity #2
Preview the study questions for Reading Assignment 9 with students. What additional predictions can students make about what might happen in this section of the book?

Activity #3
Have students read Reading Assignment 9 in whatever way you think is best: orally, silently, in pairs, or in small groups.

Activity #4
Show students a short (5 minutes or so) video about Monarch butterflies. There are several good ones on the Internet (youtube.com or elsewhere). Follow up by having students write a descriptive paragraph. Here are some suggested topics for the descriptive paragraph(s):
- Describe the life cycle of a Monarch butterfly.
- Describe a Monarch butterfly to someone who has never seen one.
- Describe how it would feel to be among the butterflies in the butterfly trees.
- Describe what thousands of Monarch butterflies look like when they're all together.

Dear Mr. Henshaw
Vocabulary For Reading Assignment 9

ANTIQUE

"I had started down the street past the paint store and *antique* shops and all those places..."(Page 81)

You probably already know what an *antique* is; it is a thing that is considered to be old and valuable, either in terms of dollar value or historical value.

Perhaps you have seen the popular television series *Antique Roadshow* or something similar, in which people bring their old treasures to be appraised (to find out how much it is worth).

What's the difference between *antique* and *old*?
Can a person be an antique?
Use antique in a sentence of your own.

_____

Dear Mr. Henshaw
Vocabulary For Reading Assignment 9

MOLEST

There was a big sign that said WARNING. $500 FINE FOR MOLESTING BUTTERFLIES IN ANY WAY. I had to smile. Who would want to molest a butterfly? (Page 82)

Think about the context. Do you think molesting is a good thing or a bad thing? What would you guess it means?

Have you ever heard this word used in another way? In the context above, the word molest means to annoy or interfere with the butterflies. Molest also has a more serious meaning that goes way beyond just annoying.

Some other forms of the word are molester (the person who does the molesting), molestation (the act of molesting), molested (past tense), and molests (another verb form).

Molestation is not a good thing. Molesters are often fined or sent to jail. A person who molests butterflies doesn't care about them, though a person who has molested a butterfly may be sorry.

Use a form of the word molest in a sentence of your own.

Dear Mr. Henshaw
Vocabulary For Reading Assignment 9

QUIVERING

"The sticks began to move, and slowly they opened wings and turned into orange and black butterflies, thousands of them quivering on one tree."(Page 82)

Quivering probably means

making small, fast movements   sleeping   resting

Synonyms are words that mean about the same thing. Synonyms for quivering would be trembling, shaking, or vibrating.

What's are the differences between trembling, shaking, vibrating, and quivering? Explore the subtle differences among these words.

Use quivering in a sentence of your own.
_____

Dear Mr. Henshaw
Vocabulary For Reading Assignment 9

WEIRD

"All the boys in my class are writing **weird** stories full of monsters, lasers and creatures from outer space."(Page 85)

Weird means "strange," "unusual," or "odd."

This is another spelling word. Usually the spelling rule is "i before e, except after c," but the word **weird** is an exception to that rule.

List several things you think are **weird**.

A person who does weird things is sometimes called a *weirdo*. A slang use of the word also includes saying something "weirded me out," meaning something made the person feel strange or perhaps afraid.

Write a definition of the word **weird**.

_____

STUDY QUESTIONS
Dear Mr. Henshaw Reading Assignment 9

Reading Assignment 9 (February 6-February 9)

1. When Leigh gets to school on February 6, what does he first notice? What does his observation lead him to believe?

2. When Leigh asks to be excused to go to the bathroom, does he really have to go? What is his intent?

3. How does Mr. Fridley keep Leigh out of trouble?

4. What gets Leigh out of his rotten mood after school?

5. What information does Chuck give Leigh to think about?

6. Why do you think Leigh is upset when his father sends him the twenty-dollar bill?

LESSON NINETEEN
Dear Mr. Henshaw

Objectives
1. Students will review the main events and ideas from Reading Assignment 9
2. Students will review literary genres.
3. Students will preview the vocabulary words for Reading Assignment 10: *villains, grateful, insulated, fastening, demonstration, muffle,* and *prowls*.
4. Students will preview the Study Questions for and read Reading Assignment 10.

Activity #1
Discuss the answers to the Study Questions for Reading Assignment 9. Put students in 6 groups, one for each question. Each group should discuss and come up with an answer for the assigned question. Then, come back together as a class to discuss all of the questions.

Activity #2
Leigh is trying to write a fictional story for the Young Writers' Yearbook. Review genres of literature. Leigh's story is *The Ten-Foot Wax Man*. Other boys in his class are writing about monsters, lasers, and creatures from outer space. Ask students what genres these kinds of stories might fit into. [fantasy, science-fiction, horror]

Take a few minutes to review the elements of fiction. Ask students what a fiction story needs to have in it. [character, setting, plot, theme, conflict] Discuss each of these elements to make sure students understand what each is. If this is new material, spend more time on it. If it is a review, just give it a quick review.

Activity #3
Preview the vocabulary words for Reading Assignment 10. Students will probably be familiar with some of the words. Some are chosen for spelling; some are chosen to discuss variations in meanings or word forms.

Activity #4
Tell students that prior to the next class meeting they should complete Reading Assignment 10, including previewing the Study Questions for Reading Assignment 10 prior to reading it. Give students the remainder of this class time to work on this assignment.

Dear Mr. Henshaw
Vocabulary For Reading Assignment 10

VILLAINS

"The boys in my class who are writing about monsters just bring in a new monster on the last page to finish off the villains with a laser." (Page 89)

Villains is a word that isn't used much anymore. Now, they are mostly referred to as "the bad guys." In studying literature, they are often called "antagonists," though antagonists don't always have to be villains.

The dictionary definition of villains says they are devoted to wickedness or crime. They are evil, which would make sense. Look at the first part of the word: "vil" is part of evil. Villains are evil people.

Look in a dictionary to find some synonyms for the word villain.

Think of some movies you have seen. Name the movies and the characters who are villains.

Dear Mr. Henshaw
Vocabulary For Reading Assignment 10

GRATEFUL

Leigh signs his February 28th entry "Your grateful friend." (Page 91)

Grate is an obsolete word (from the 1500's) that meant "agreeable" or "thankful." It came from the Latin word *gratus*, which means "pleasing."

The suffix -ful means "full of." So, grateful literally means "full of thankful."

How is the word grateful different from the word *thankful*? One is usually grateful for personal favors or help whereas we're usually thankful for things. Grateful is a warmer, more personal or humble expression of thanks or appreciation.

What are you grateful for?

I am grateful for _____.

Dear Mr. Henshaw
Vocabulary For Reading Assignment 10

INSULATED

"While I was looking around for the right kind of **insulated** wire, a man who had been watching me...."(Page 94)

Here is another word of Latin origin. The Latin word *insulatus* meant "make into an island." If you think about insulated wire, the wire has been made into an island, surrounded and cut off from the outside world.

If people are is **insulated**, they live in a place cut off from the rest of the world, like an island. Or one could say that monks live an **insulated** life, away on a mountain top in their own community.

Thermos jugs are **insulated**; the insides are surrounded by foam or other materials that help hold in the heat or cold.

You may have boots that **insulate** your feet, surrounding them with a warm lining and a waterproof shell.

> What other things can you think of that are **insulated**?

> Why would some kinds of wire need to be **insulated**?

Dear Mr. Henshaw
Vocabulary For Reading Assignment 10

FASTENING

"Then I went to work **fastening** one wire from the battery to the switch and from the other side of the switch to the doorbell." (Page 97)

Based on the context of the sentence above, what does **fastening** mean?

       attaching   working quickly   enveloping

Fastening is a sneaky word because the "t" is silent. When you say it, you skip over the "t," but when you write it, you have to remember to put it in.

This isn't a word with Latin roots, it's Old English from the word *faest*, meaning "firmly fixed." Did your grandmother ever tell you to "hold fast to my hand" as you crossed a street? She wanted you to stick right with her. Think of being "fast asleep." This "fast" doesn't have to do with speed; rather, with being firmly fixed.

    What kinds of **fasteners** can you think of? List them here.

Dear Mr. Henshaw
Vocabulary For Reading Assignment 10

DEMONSTRATION

"I let her in and gave her a **demonstration** of my burglar alarm."(Page 98)

Even though the word "demon" is in demonstration, it doesn't have to do with evil spirits!

If you give a **demonstration** of something, what do you do?

Demonstration comes from the Latin (again!), from *de-* (which means "entirely") and *monstrare* (which means *to point out* or *to show*).

Demonstration is a noun, a thing. The demonstration was successful. There are other forms of the word. To demonstrate is the verb form; it shows action. Leigh demonstrated the burglar alarm for his mother.

Make up three sentences, each using a different form of the word demonstration.

_____

_____

_____

Dear Mr. Henshaw
Vocabulary For Reading Assignment 10

MUFFLE

"Would my sandwich **muffle** the bell?" (Page 98)

What do you think the word **muffle** means?

squish   make dirty   make less noisy

Have you ever heard of a **muffler**? It's a part of a car or truck. What does it do?

Do you wear ear **muffs**? What do they do?

How can these words be related? Ear muffs keep your ears warm, but a muffler keeps a car quieter. Seems like they have nothing in common until you think about it for a minute. What do they all have in common?

We have the Dutch, from the French, from the Latin to thank for these words. A "muff" is an old-fashioned mitten. It is a tube-shaped piece of cloth or fur about 12" to 18" long into which people would put their hands to keep them warm. If you would stick something noisy in there, the sound would be "**muffled**," covered up and made less noisy.

Dear Mr. Henshaw
Vocabulary For Reading Assignment 10

PROWLS

"The principal, who always prowls around keeping an eye on things at lunchtime, came over to examine my lunchbox."(Page 101)

What does prowls mean, based on the context above?

      sits   skips   hunts   walks

This is an important word choice that Beverly Cleary makes. She could have chosen "walks" or "sneaks" or "scoots" or "visits," or lots of other words, but she chose prowls. Why?

It has to do with the connotation of the word prowls. Prowling is to go stealthily, as a cat hunting a mouse or a thief looking for an opportunity to steal something. It has a negative connotation of being sneaky with a motive. It gives us the idea that the principal is not friendly; he's looking to catch somebody in the act of doing something wrong.

Compare and contrast this image of the principal with the image we have of Mr. Fridley.

Use a form of the word prowls in a sentence of your own.

STUDY QUESTIONS ANSWER KEY
Dear Mr. Henshaw Reading Assignment 9

Reading Assignment 9 (February 6-February 9)
1. When Leigh gets to school on February 6, what does he first notice? What does his observation lead him to believe?

    Leigh notices that Mr. Fridley has already put up the flag (with the bear right side up). He thinks that perhaps Mr. Fridley doesn't really need his help, after all.

2. When Leigh asks to be excused to go to the bathroom, does he really have to go? What is his intent?

    Leigh does not need to use the bathroom. He's mad and wants to get out of class. He intends to kick down the hall the lunch he grabbed on his way out the door, just to get even at somebody for stealing his cheesecake.

3. How does Mr. Fridley keep Leigh out of trouble?

    Mr. Fridley sees Leigh and asks him what he thinks he's doing. He tells Leigh he doesn't want to see Leigh get into trouble, tells him everybody has problems, and advises him to find a way to remain positive if he wants to have friends. Mr. Fridley gives Leigh a little shove towards his classroom, and Leigh goes back.

4. What gets Leigh out of his rotten mood after school?

    Leigh goes for a walk and visits the butterfly trees.

5. What information does Chuck give Leigh to think about?

    Chuck tells Leigh that the Alarm System box has batteries and a bell.

6. Why do you think Leigh is upset when his father sends him the twenty-dollar bill?

    He thinks his father doesn't understand his feelings and isn't really sorry about losing Bandit.

STUDY QUESTIONS
Dear Mr. Henshaw Reading Assignment 10

Reading Assignment 10 (February 15-March 15)
1. Why does Leigh get behind in his diary writing?

2. What does Leigh buy with the twenty dollars that his father sends him?

3. How does Leigh's burglar alarm change things for Leigh at school?

4. Why is Leigh glad that he didn't catch the "lunchbox thief"?

5. How does Leigh feel about his burglar alarm invention?

LESSON TWENTY
Dear Mr. Henshaw

Objectives
1. Students will review the main events and ideas from Reading Assignment 10.
2. Students will discuss the symbolism of Leigh's wax man.
3. Students will learn about allusion and explore the allusion in the March 15th entry.
4. Students will discuss Leigh's difficulty with endings in this section of the book.
5. Students will compare the adult male characters in *Dear Mr. Henshaw*.
6. Students will explore one way of creating descriptive sentences.
7. Students will practice quick-writing on a number of different topics.
8. Students will review the vocabulary words introduced so far in this unit.

Activity #1
Discuss the answers to the Study Questions for Reading Assignment 10.

Activity #2
Conduct selected discussions and activities from the Additional Points notes that follow this lesson plan. The objectives for this lesson include items from all of the Additional Points for Discussion & Activities for this section of the book. You may do all of them or pick-and-choose which ones you would like to cover.

Activity #3
Distribute Dear Mr. Henshaw Crossword Puzzle 2. Give students ample time to complete it (perhaps overnight if necessary), then display the answers so students can check their own work. This is a review of the vocabulary words covered in Reading Assignments 1-10.

STUDY QUESTIONS ANSWER KEY
Dear Mr. Henshaw Reading Assignment 10

Reading Assignment 10 (February 15-March 15)

1. Why does Leigh get behind in his diary writing?
    He is working on his story, he is writing to Mr. Henshaw, and he has to buy a new notebook because he has filled up the first one.

2. What does Leigh buy with the twenty dollars that his father sends him?
    Leigh buys things to make his "burglar alarm" for his lunch box.

3. How does Leigh's burglar alarm change things for Leigh at school?
    He gets positive attention from the other students and even from the principal due to his invention. He starts to feel that he is not so "medium" after all.

4. Why is Leigh glad that he didn't catch the "lunchbox thief"?
    He is glad he didn't catch the "lunchbox thief" because if the thief had set off the alarm in the classroom, the thief would have been in big trouble, and Leigh didn't want to get anyone in trouble since he had to go to school with whomever it was. He just wanted his lunch every day.

5. How does Leigh feel about his burglar alarm invention?
    He is excited and proud that the invention worked, and he is excited that others liked, and some even copied, his invention.

ADDITIONAL POINTS FOR DISCUSSION AND ACTIVITIES
Dear Mr. Henshaw, Reading Assignment 10

Symbolism

Leigh chooses to write a story about a ten-foot-tall truck driver made of wax, who melts a little each time he crosses the desert. Talk with students a little bit about the possible symbolism of this choice.

A ten-foot-tall truck driver is a larger-than-life character (like maybe Paul Bunyan or Superman). We would expect him to be strong and manly...but this ten-foot-man is made of wax. That's really odd. Who would think of that! Talk with students about how when kids are little their parents are sometimes "larger than life," almost "super heroes" to them. Leigh seems to almost idolize his dad. Then, Leigh starts to learn about his dad's less-than-heroic traits: he doesn't call when he says he will; he tells white lies; he loses the dog; he has another family. With each passing day, each passing week, Leigh's dad, like the wax man, melts away and gets smaller in Leigh's estimation. Explain to students how the wax man of Leigh's story is symbolic of Leigh's estimation of his own father.

<u>Follow-up</u>: Invite students to do a quick-write or journal entry about someone they do or did look up to and how their perceptions have changed over time (if they have), either for the better or worse.

Endings: Winners and Losers and Satisfaction

Endings are problematic for Leigh in this section of the book. Bringing in a new monster to kill off the villain at the end of the story doesn't seem right to him. Having someone turn up to make candles of his wax man at the end doesn't work for him. And, he's having trouble finishing a letter thanking his father for the $20.

Ask your students, "Why don't the suggested endings feel right to Leigh?". [Leigh wants there to be a "winner." He wants there to be a hero who wins in the end. A monster brought in at the last minute to kill the villain is not the hero one has been connected with through the story. The wax truck driver should be the hero, but he is melted into a useless thing. These aren't satisfying endings for Leigh.]

Why can't Leigh finish the letter to his father? [The $20 "gift" is an unsatisfactory ending to the losing of Bandit story. Leigh wants Bandit, not $20. Leigh wants his father to be responsible, to not have lost the dog in the first place. An irresponsible father and no dog is bad enough, but sending $20 to "make up" for losing Bandit is lame on top of that. A personal visit, a ride in the truck and an in-person apology would have meant so much more than sending $20. The $20 doesn't make it all right, and it's hard to write a thank you note for something which is unsatisfying, something for which one is not truly grateful.]

Dear Mr. Henshaw Additional Points For Discussion & Activities Reading Assignment 10 Page 2

Character Comparisons
Ask students what they think of the man at the hardware store. Is he kind? Intuitive? Helpful? Mean? Short-tempered? Likeable? Was he prowling around his store the way the principal prowled around the cafeteria?

Talk about the strengths and weaknesses of each of the adult male characters in the book: Leigh's dad, Mr. Fridley, the principal, and the hardware store man.

Follow-up: After the discussion, have students do a quick-write character sketch of any one of these characters.

Descriptive Sentences
Tell students: Leigh says, "Barry lives in a big old house that is sort of cheerful and messy, with little girls all over the place." In one sentence, we have a really vivid picture of Barry's house. How does Beverly Cleary do that? [She taps into our background knowledge–memories–of cheerful houses and messy houses and what little girls are like running around, which elicits a pool of information and a combination of mental images that almost instantly give us a feeling for Barry's house.] Discuss student answers and show them how this works. Write some descriptive sentences together as a class.

Follow-up: Have students write a one-sentence description of a home they are familiar with...their own, a friend's, a relative's...using the same technique Beverly Cleary uses.

Allusion
Your students may not yet have been introduced to allusion. If not, introduce them to it, explaining what it is [a reference in the story to something outside of the book]. A good example of allusion is in the March 15th entry: "You know that song about the hills ringing with the sound of music? Well, you might say our cafeteria rang with the sound of burglar alarms."

To what is Leigh referring? [He's referring to *The Sound of Music*, a movie about the VonTrapp family, starring Julie Andrews. The movie opens with the Julie Andrews character, Maria, out in the hills of the Alps singing, "The hills are alive with the sound of music."]

Follow-up: Play the Sound of Music song for your students. Invite them to watch the film together after school or one evening...or individually for extra credit.

VOCABULARY REVIEW CROSSWORD 1
Dear Mr. Henshaw

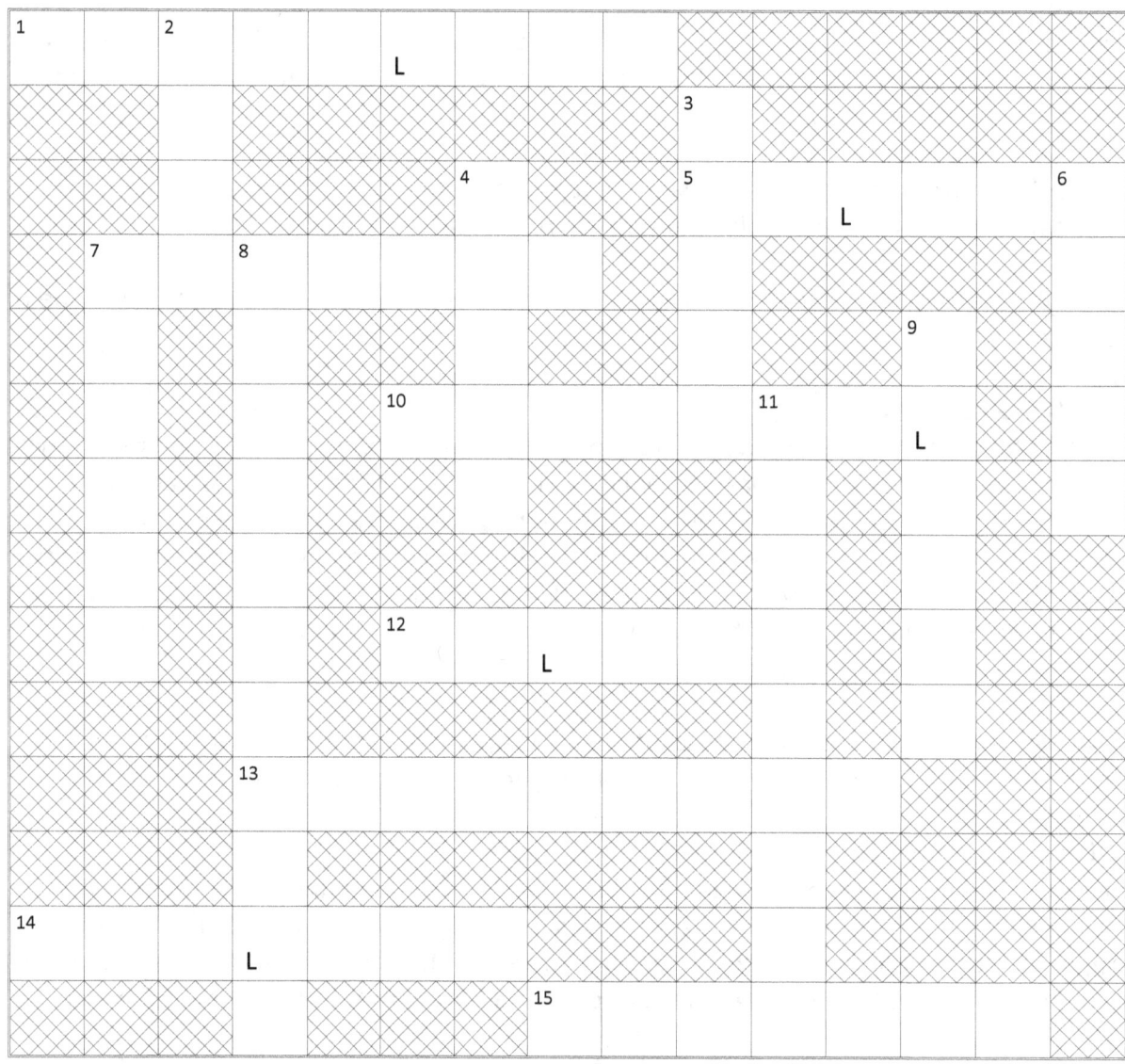

Across
1. Moving at high speed
5. A kind of fungus
7. Came to a conclusion after thinking about something
10. Thankful
12. To bother or interfere with
13. As determined by or in keeping with
14. Transporting as with a truck or cart
15. Scolding, complaining, or constantly finding fault

Down
2. Having bad manners
3. To occupy in an agreeable, pleasing, or entertaining way
4. Strange; bizarre; sometimes involving the supernatural
6. Strong anger
7. Very dry region
8. At ease; relaxed
9. Skin or other tissue break-down
11. Attaching

VOCABULARY REVIEW CROSSWORD 1 ANSWER KEY
Dear Mr. Henshaw

	1 B	A	2 R	R	E	L	I	N	G				
			U							3 A			
			D				4 W		5 M	I	L	D	6 E W
		7 D	E	8 C	I	D	E	D		U			R
			E		O		I			S		9 U	A
			S		M		10 G	R	A	T	11 E F	U	L	T
			E		F			D			A		C	H
			R		O						S		E	
			T		R		12 M	O	L	E	S	T		R	
					T						E		S	
				13 A	C	C	O	R	D	I	N	G	
				B							I	
	14 H	A	U	L	I	N	G				N	
				E			15 N	A	G	G	I	N	G

Across
1. Moving at high speed
5. A kind of fungus
7. Came to a conclusion after thinking about something
10. Thankful
12. To bother or interfere with
13. As determined by or in keeping with
14. Transporting as with a truck or cart
15. Scolding, complaining, or constantly finding fault

Down
2. Having bad manners
3. To occupy in an agreeable, pleasing, or entertaining way
4. Strange; bizarre; sometimes involving the supernatural
6. Strong anger
7. Very dry region
8. At ease; relaxed
9. Skin or other tissue break-down
11. Attaching

LESSON TWENTY-ONE
Dear Mr. Henshaw

Objectives
1. Students will read Reading Assignment 11 in class.
2. Students will collaborate to determine and discuss the most important events in this section of the book.
3. Students will determine the main ideas in each dated entry of Reading Assignment and create one study question for each main idea.
4. Students will lead a class discussion and take notes for studying purposes.
5. Students will read Reading Assignment 12.

NOTE: Vocabulary words and worksheets are available for Reading Assignments 11 & 12 if you choose to use them. They are not planned for use in these lessons.

Activity #1
Today, things will be a little backwards. We've been previewing vocabulary words and study questions prior to reading throughout most of the book. Today, students will jump right into reading Reading Assignment 11. How students do this is up to you—orally, silently, pairs, groups. To do the next activity students need to have completed the reading, so you may want to have them read orally...or maybe you would read the section to them while they follow along...just so everyone finishes at the same time. That's up to you.

Activity #2
After students have finished reading this section of the book, break them into groups and assign each group one of the dated entries. Each group should make a list of the most important things in its section and develop one study question for each item. There should only be 1 to 3 questions for each group; the point is to get them to pick out the main ideas and to think through them enough to create good questions. Make sure students understand that we're not after minute details or "tricky" questions. Students can refer to other study questions for other Reading Assignments to see the types of questions to ask.

Activity #3
When all the groups are finished, have each group lead a discussion of its entry. Students should take notes for studying purposes. Help students with note-taking as much or as little as needed. You may want to compile the questions and answers into a handout to give out at the beginning of your next class meeting.

Activity #4
Tell students that prior to the next class meeting, they should finish reading *Dear Mr. Henshaw*—the final reading assignment.

LESSON TWENTY-TWO
Dear Mr. Henshaw

Objectives
1. Students will review the main ideas and events from Reading Assignment 12.
2. Students will discuss several passages from Reading Assignment 12 to gain a better understanding of the characters and themes.

Activity #1
Review the main ideas and events from Reading Assignment 12 by discussing the Study Questions for this section together as a whole class.

Activity #2
Following this daily lesson is a page of quotations taken from this section of the book. Have your students prepare explanations about what each of these passages shows or why it is important. Assigning one or two passages to small groups of students for them to discuss would probably be the best way to approach this work. Follow up with a whole-class discussion of all of the passages.

This completes the reading and discussions for each of the individual Reading Assignments for *Dear Mr. Henshaw*. The lessons which follow are geared towards studying the elements of fiction throughout the whole book: character, theme, conflict, plot, and symbolism.

STUDY QUESTIONS
Dear Mr. Henshaw Reading Assignment 12

Reading Assignment 10 (March 25-March 31)

1. What does Mrs. Badger like best about "A Day on Dad's Rig"?

2. What does Leigh's story win in the Young Writer's Contest?

3. Who is Angela Badger?

4. How does Mrs. Badger describe Mr. Henshaw?

5. How does Leigh feel when Mrs. Badger calls him an author?

6. How does Leigh's dad find Bandit?

7. Why does Leigh give Bandit back to his father?

STUDY QUESTIONS ANSWER KEY
Dear Mr. Henshaw Reading Assignment 12

Reading Assignment 12 (March 25-March 31)
1. What does Mrs. Badger like best about "A Day on Dad's Rig"?
    Mrs. Badger likes "A Day on Dad's Rig" because "it was written by a boy who wrote honestly about something he knew and had strong feelings about."

2. What does Leigh's story win in the Young Writer's Contest?
    Leigh's story wins an honorable mention.

3. Who is Angela Badger?
    She is a real author with whom Leigh gets to have lunch. She calls Leigh a "real author." She also has met Mr. Henshaw.

4. How does Mrs. Badger describe Mr. Henshaw?
    She describes him as "a very nice young man with a wicked twinkle in his eye."

5. How does Leigh feel when Mrs. Badger calls him an author?
    He is a little embarrassed, but he is very proud.

6. How does Leigh's dad find Bandit?
    He asks every day over his CB radio and finally gets an answer from a trucker who has picked up a lost dog in a snowstorm in the Sierra. They meet at a weigh station, and Bandit is returned to Leigh's dad.

7. Why does Leigh give Bandit back to his father?
    Leigh thinks his father needs Bandit more than he does, and Leigh has no way to keep Bandit amused. Leigh thought Bandit would be happier with his father.

PASSAGES FOR DISCUSSION
Dear Mr. Henshaw, Reading Assignment 12

Consider the following passages from Reading Assignment 12 of *Dear Mr. Henshaw* and explain why each is important.

1. I don't like to think about Dad being lonesome, but I don't like to think about the pizza boy cheering him up, either. (Page 111)

2. "Your father isn't a bad man by any means." (Page 112)

3. Some kids were mad because they didn't win or even get something printed. They said they wouldn't ever try to write again which I think is pretty dumb. I have heard that real authors sometimes have their books turned down. I figure you win some, you lose some. (Page 114)

4. She called me an author. *A real live author called me an author.* (Page 119)

5. I didn't think answers to those questions were very important. (Page 120)

6. Dad's stomach hung over his belt, and he wasn't as tall as I remembered him. (Page 128)

7. After all these months when I had longed to see him, it took a load of broccoli to get him here. I felt let down and my feelings hurt. (Page 129)

8. He rumpled my hair and said, "You're smarter than your old man." That embarrassed me. I didn't know how to answer. (Page 130)

9. "So long, son," he said. "I'll try to get over to see you more often."
"Sure, Dad," I said. I had learned by now that I couldn't count on anything he said. (Page 132)

10. "Dad, you keep Bandit. You need him more than I do. ... Please take him. I don't have any way to amuse him." (Page 133)

PASSAGES FOR DISCUSSION SUGGESTED ANSWERS
Dear Mr. Henshaw, Reading Assignment 12

Consider the following passages from Reading Assignment 12 of *Dear Mr. Henshaw* and explain why each is important.

1. I don't like to think about Dad being lonesome, but I don't like to think about the pizza boy cheering him up, either. (Page 111)

   Leigh is grown up enough to understand his dad is probably lonesome without a family but he isn't grown up enough to let his dad go and do whatever makes his dad happy. This passage shows Leigh's state of being in between a kid and an adult.

2. "Your father isn't a bad man by any means." (Page 112)

   It seems like the divorce was fairly amicable. It's clear that Leigh's mom doesn't hate his dad or harbor ill-will towards him. In fact, she sees him pretty objectively and tries to help Leigh see him that way, too. This objective nurturing is important for Leigh.

3. Some kids were mad because they didn't win or even get something printed. They said they wouldn't ever try to write again which I think is pretty dumb. I have heard that real authors sometimes have their books turned down. I figure you win some, you lose some. (Page 114)

   We think of little kids as getting pouty and mad. Leigh rises above that and sees that rejection is a part of life; you just deal with it and move on or try again. This passage once more shows Leigh's maturity.

4. She called me an author. *A real live author called me an author.* (Page 119)

   Although Leigh is mature in many ways, he is still a kid who is impressed by things and needs reinforcement from others. He sees himself as a "medium" sort of person. That makes him humble and appreciative of compliments from others he sees as better than himself.

5. I didn't think answers to those questions were very important. (Page 120)

   The questions the girls were asking were the typical questions that an author probably is always asked by all of her fans. Leigh is not very interested in the author's books—in fact, he hasn't read any of them—so these kinds of questions don't interest him much either. Being a little more mature than his classmates, Leigh seems to tend to like deeper or not the usual information, and he doesn't think these questions are important.

Dear Mr. Henshaw Passages For Discussion Suggested Answers Reading Assignment 12 Page 2

6. Dad's stomach hung over his belt, and he wasn't as tall as I remembered him. (Page 128)
   Leigh tends to think of his father how he wants his father to be instead of how he actually is, though he is learning about the reality of his father's ways. Here Leigh is face-to-face with reality, and he recognizes that reality is different from what has been in his thoughts.

7. After all these months when I had longed to see him, it took a load of broccoli to get him here. I felt let down and my feelings hurt. (Page 129)
   Leigh wants to be more important than a load of broccoli to his father.

8. He rumpled my hair and said, "You're smarter than your old man." That embarrassed me. I didn't know how to answer. (Page 130)
   Leigh wants his dad to be his hero. When his dad indicates that Leigh is smarter than he is, Leigh, somewhere deep inside, probably recognizes that it's true—but he doesn't want to be smarter than the person he wants to be his hero. What do you say when reality hits you and you realize your dream is wrong? Leigh can't think of anything to say.

9. "So long, son," he said. "I'll try to get over to see you more often."
"Sure, Dad," I said. I had learned by now that I couldn't count on anything he said. (Page 132)
   It's interesting that Leigh's dad finally calls him "son." Later in this scene, he actually calls him by name, "Leigh." This passage is really more about Leigh's father's character development than Leigh's. At the time when Leigh is finally accepting that his dad is not dependable and that he (Leigh) is no more important than a load of broccoli, we outsiders can see that maybe (just maybe) Leigh's dad is finally starting to grow up. Leigh's father seems to genuinely want to reunite and to be a part of his son's life.

10. "Dad, you keep Bandit. You need him more than I do. ... Please take him. I don't have any way to amuse him." (Page 133)
    Leigh has grown up some more. He would like to have Bandit at home, but he wants his dad to have the dog for companionship. He even goes so far as to tell a white lie to get his dad to take the dog. Leigh's favorite book is *Ways to Amuse a Dog*; surely, he has ways to amuse Bandit. He is just trying to find something to say to get his dad to take the dog.

ELEMENTS OF FICTION: CHARACTER
Dear Mr. Henshaw

Activity

Decide if you want students to work individually or in small groups to do this assignment. Assign each student (or group) a main character from *Dear Mr. Henshaw*: Leigh, Leigh's mom, Leigh's dad, Mr. Henshaw, or Mr. Fridley. Students should complete the Character Traits graphic organizer for their assigned characters.

When the graphic organizers are completed, come together as a class to discuss the characters, their traits, and the supporting evidence for students' trait choices.

Follow-up: There are a number of different possibilities for additional, related assignments or activities:
- Write a character sketch of one character, based on the information on the graphic organizer.
- Compare and contrast a variety of character combinations: Mr. Fridley/the principal; Leigh's mom/Angela Badger; Mr. Fridley/Leigh's dad; Leigh/Barry.
- Write a persuasive essay convincing Leigh that his dad is finally growing up.
- Leigh's mom is studying to be a nurse. Explain why she will probably be a very good nurse based on evidence in the story. What traits does a good nurse have? How does Leigh's mom exhibit those traits?
- Discuss the role/use of each of the minor characters in the story: Bandit, Miss Martinez, Katy, the principal, the hardware store man, the trucker who delivered the jacket, Angela Badger, Barry, and the school librarian. Choose a symbol for each minor character and explain your choice.
- Role play. Mr. Fridley meets Leigh's mom at school; Angela Badger talks to Leigh's dad about Leigh's writing work; Barry's mom talks to Leigh's mom; the librarian talks to Anglea Badger about Leigh; Mr. Fridley talks to Leigh's teacher about the stolen lunch problem; Katy and Leigh's mom talk about Leigh; Leigh has lunch with Mr. Henshaw; Mr. Henshaw talks with Angela Badger about Leigh
- Cast the characters for a movie of the book and justify your choices.
- Describe Leigh through poetry.
- You are Leigh's friend. Write a letter to Mr. Henshaw persuading him to come visit Leigh.
- Discussion: Does Mr. Henshaw give Leigh good advice?
- We never see the notes/cards/letters Mr. Henshaw writes to Leigh. Have your students write each of Mr. Henshaw's notes/cards/letters.

ELEMENTS OF FICTION - CHARACTER TRAITS
Dear Mr. Henshaw

In the small circle, write your character's name. In each larger circle, write one character trait and give an example of that trait from the story.

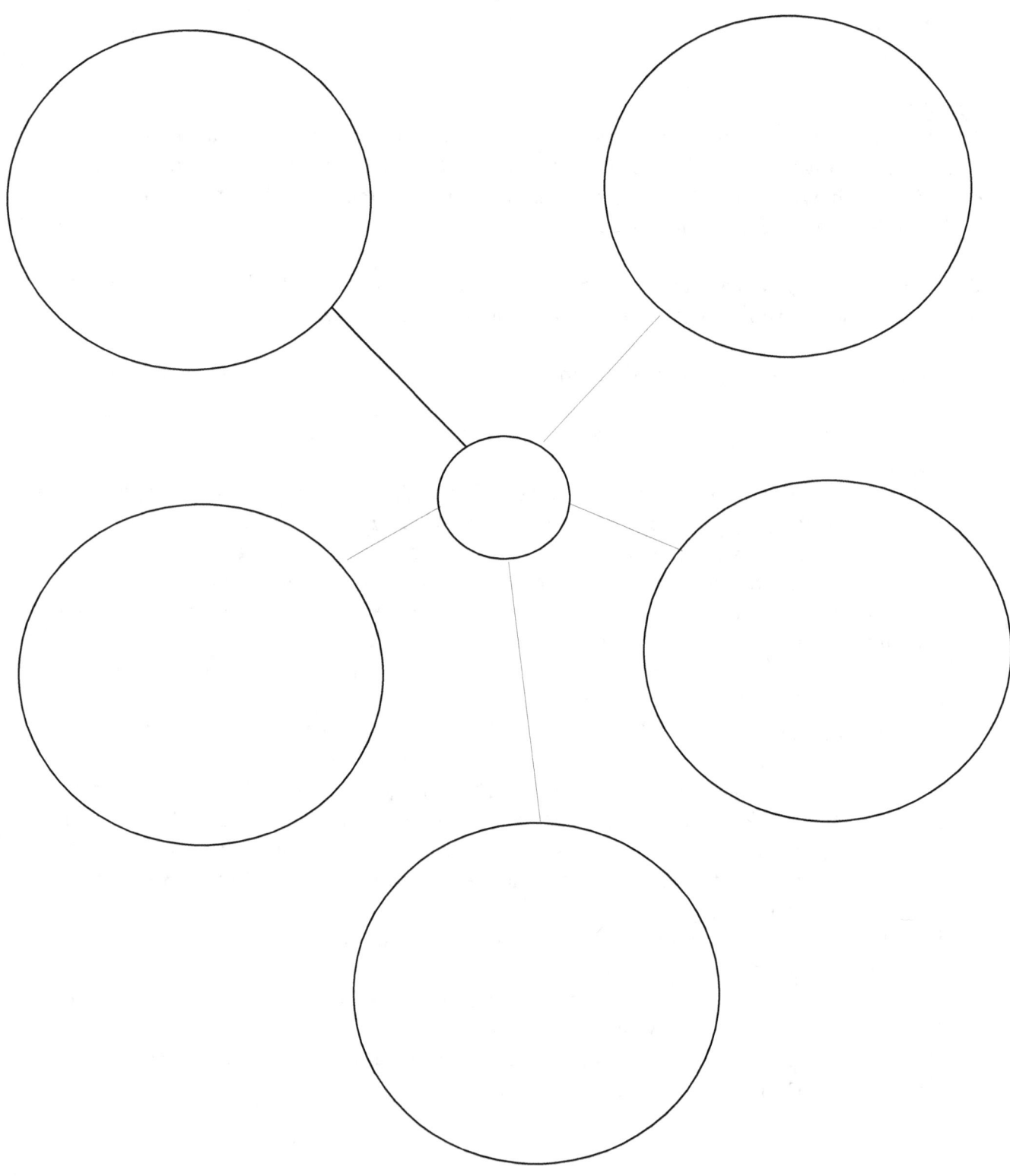

ELEMENTS OF FICTION: THEMES
Dear Mr. Henshaw

Activity #1
There are many themes and motifs in *Dear Mr. Henshaw*.

Get as many blank sheets of paper as there are students in your class plus a couple of extras. Write each of the following on one sheet of paper: loneliness, friendship, the power of writing, economic hardship, divorce, believing in yourself, growing up, loss, illusion vs reality, and nurturing. Repeat until all the blank sheets have a theme written on them. Crumple up the papers, each into a wad, and put them in a medium-sized, clean trash can.

- Hand the trash can to a student.
- The student should pull out one wad of paper, uncrumple it, and read what it says.
- The student should then give an example of something exhibiting that theme in the book.
- The student then takes the trash can to another student in the class and the process is repeated.

When all students have had a turn, put the trash can in the middle of the room and let students re-crumple their papers and shoot baskets to return the themes to the basket. Repeat if time permits.

Activity #2
Write the list of themes where students can see them. Ask students to (silently) choose which idea in the book they most related to. Have students do a quick-write explaining why they connected with the themes they chose.

Follow-up: Any of these would be good follow-up activities or assignments.
- Have students choose one theme or motif and write an essay about that theme in *Dear Mr. Henshaw*.
- Have an author come in to talk about the power of writing and his/her experiences with getting published.
- Ask students if any of the themes in Dear Mr. Henshaw are a part of any other books they have read. A writing assignment would be to compare how the theme is handled in each book.
- Let students work in small groups, with each group focusing on a different theme, to come up with one sentence that would best summarize that theme in the story.

ELEMENTS OF FICTION: CONFLICT
Dear Mr. Henshaw

Activity #1
Review the types of conflicts with your students: person vs. person, person vs. self, person vs. society, person vs. nature, person vs. fate/God, person vs. technology. See if students can give you examples of each. If not, help them along with further explanations and examples.

Activity #2
Have students fill out the Conflict Chart. Again, you choose the most appropriate method for your students–individually, in pairs or small groups, or as a whole class. If you don't do it as a whole class, save time for discussing students' responses.

Follow-up: Here are some other activities you could choose to do if you want to spend more time on conflict.

- **Conflict Resolution** One of the main conflicts in the story is person vs. person, Bonnie vs. Bill. If Bill really wants to get back together with Bonnie, what will he have to do to resolve the conflict? First define the conflict and then pose solutions. Broaden the discussion to talk about ways to get along with others–how to recognize problems and think through solutions.
- **Belonging** One of Leigh's conflicts is trying to fit in at school. Discuss with students the ways Leigh tries to become a part of things at his new school. Have students write or make video shorts of advice to Leigh, suggestions for ways to become a part of school life and make new friends.
- **Related Conflicts** Leigh's biggest problem at school is the lunch thief. Have students discuss what some other common conflicts are that happen at school--and ways to resolve each. Students could make a video presentation of common problems and post the video on your school's website to help new students.
- **Role Play** Leigh is hurt and frustrated by his father's irresponsibility, as was Bonnie. Role play a conversation between Leigh and his dad in which Leigh talks to his dad about his feelings and frustrations. Discuss with students whether they think this kind of a conversation would/could help bring any kind of resolution to the conflict.
- **Write A Letter** Have students write a letter to someone with whom they are frustrated or by whom they have been hurt, expressing their feelings and posing solutions. On the other hand, if they know they are frustrating or have hurt someone else, they could write a letter to that person apologizing or offering an explanation and/or solution.

ELEMENTS OF FICTION - CONFLICT CHART
Dear Mr. Henshaw

Under each column, give examples of that type of conflict in *Dear Mr. Henshaw*. Be prepared to explain how the conflict applies to your example.

person vs. person	person vs. self	person vs. nature	person vs. technology

person vs. person	person vs. self	person vs. nature	person vs. society

ELEMENTS OF FICTION: PLOT
Dear Mr. Henshaw

Activity #1
For such a small book, there's a lot going on in Dear Mr. Henshaw. Try to get your students to pull out (list) the different plot parts that run throughout the book. Here is a suggested list for you:
- Past family life together
- Leigh's relationship with Mr. Henshaw
- Becoming a writer
- Trying to catch the lunch thief
- Making friends
- Leigh's relationship with his dad
- Relationship of Bonnie & Bill
- Bandit
- Leigh's relationship with Mr. Fridley

Activity #2
Here are some discussion questions about the plot.
- Which of these story elements is considered the main story line? Why?
- What does each of these parts of the plot add to the story? Realism? Mystery? Warmth? Conflict? ...or? Look at each part of the plot and determine what it adds.

Activity #3
Talk with students about the format of the book. Here are some discussion questions:
- Did using letters and diary entries make it easier or harder to weave all of the plot elements into the story?
- All the plot elements were told from Leigh's point of view. How might the book have been different if it had been written in the 3rd person?
- What other effects does using the letter/diary entries format have on the story?

Follow-up: Here are some additional activities related to plot.
3rd Person Have students rewrite one entry in 3rd person rather than 1st person narrative. Discuss the differences between 1st and 3rd person and the problems encountered in making the change.
Predicting Have students write an opinion essay answering the question, "Will Bonnie and Bill eventually get back together again?" or "Will Leigh's dad really visit more often now?"
Sequel Have students write the plot summary of a sequel to *Dear Mr. Henshaw*.

ELEMENTS OF FICTION: SYMBOLISM
Dear Mr. Henshaw

Activity #1
We've already discussed some elements of symbolism in the story—the shoes for example. Here are a few others you might consider:

- Leigh's lunch is missing items; Leigh's family is missing a piece. Leigh really wants the good parts of his lunch, and he really wants his father to be home and a part of his daily life.

- Rainy weather at the most difficult parts of Leigh's story

- Bandit—Leigh's dad treats the dog like he treats Leigh, with little care...then at the end of the story he makes the effort to find and get Bandit, as he is making the effort to reunite with Leigh and Bonnie.

- Leigh's dad's big rig truck—as symbolic of his dad's freedom and escaping from ties as well as symbolic of Leigh's dad himself

This isn't a highly symbolic book, so no follow-up activities are really warranted. Hit the highlights and use your time in other areas.

NOTES
Dear Mr. Henshaw

MATCHING 1
Dear Mr. Henshaw

____ 1. FRIDLEY   A. Fictitious name on Leigh's lunch

____ 2. PROMISES   B. She is the Famous Author the kids met for lunch.

____ 3. KATY   C. Bonnie's catering boss

____ 4. WAX   D. Mr. Fridley sometimes guards this.

____ 5. QUESTIONS   E. State where Leigh and his mom live

____ 6. JOE   F. Leigh visits the ____ trees.

____ 7. BARRY   G. She saved Mr. Henshaw's new book for Leigh.

____ 8. CANAPES   H. Leigh first writes about a ten-foot ____ man.

____ 9. LEIGH   I. Dad doesn't keep his ____ to Leigh.

____ 10. ALASKA   J. Leigh's dog

____ 11. CALIFORNIA   K. Mr. Henshaw moves to this state that has moose.

____ 12. MONSTERS   L. Mom, Dad, and Leigh made up silly songs about these.

____ 13. CLEARY   M. Most of the boys wrote about these.

____ 14. LIBRARIAN   N. He is the protagonist, the main character in the story.

____ 15. SHOES   O. Author of Dear Mr. Henshaw

____ 16. GARBAGE   P. It signals a low point or troubling time in the story.

____ 17. BANDIT   Q. Friend from school who eats dinner with Leigh

____ 18. BADGER   R. Having to answer these made Leigh mad at first.

____ 19. BUTTERFLY   S. Special little food items for Leigh's lunch

____ 20. RAIN   T. He asks Leigh to help with the flag at school

MATCHING 2
Dear Mr. Henshaw

____ 1. BADGER   A. Dad doesn't keep his ___ to Leigh.

____ 2. CALIFORNIA   B. He is the protagonist, the main character in the story.

____ 3. MARTINEZ   C. State where Leigh and his mom live

____ 4. LEIGH   D. Christmas present from Dad

____ 5. FRIDLEY   E. Leigh visits the ___ trees.

____ 6. DIARY   F. Friend from school who eats dinner with Leigh

____ 7. BARRY   G. Fictitious name on Leigh's lunch

____ 8. JOE   H. Last name of Leigh, Bonnie, and Bill

____ 9. BOTTS   I. Bonnie's catering boss

____ 10. CLEARY   J. Leigh wants to be this when he grows up.

____ 11. HENSHAW   K. Special book Leigh writes in

____ 12. JACKET   L. Leigh's teacher

____ 13. WRITER   M. Author of Ways to Amuse a Dog

____ 14. WAX   N. Leigh's dog

____ 15. KATY   O. Mom, Dad, and Leigh made up silly songs about these.

____ 16. PROMISES   P. It signals a low point or troubling time in the story.

____ 17. BUTTERFLY   Q. Author of Dear Mr. Henshaw

____ 18. SHOES   R. Leigh first writes about a ten-foot ___ man.

____ 19. BANDIT   S. She is the Famous Author the kids met for lunch.

____ 20. RAIN   T. He asks Leigh to help with the flag at school

MATCHING 3
Dear Mr. Henshaw

____ 1. PIZZA   A. Fictitious name on Leigh's lunch

____ 2. RAIN   B. It signals a low point or troubling time in the story.

____ 3. FRIDLEY   C. Bonnie's catering boss

____ 4. BOTTS   D. She saved Mr. Henshaw's new book for Leigh.

____ 5. BUTTERFLY   E. Having to answer these made Leigh mad at first.

____ 6. CLEARY   F. Author of Dear Mr. Henshaw

____ 7. ALARM   G. Leigh visits the ___ trees.

____ 8. CANAPES   H. Leigh wants to be this when he grows up.

____ 9. LEIGH   I. Last name of Leigh, Bonnie, and Bill

____ 10. KATY   J. State where Leigh and his mom live

____ 11. LIBRARIAN   K. Mr. Fridley gave Leigh the idea for this.

____ 12. JOE   L. Special little food items for Leigh's lunch

____ 13. PROMISES   M. He is the protagonist, the main character in the story.

____ 14. CALIFORNIA   N. I wonder if Dad will marry the ___ boy and his mother.

____ 15. MARTINEZ   O. Dad doesn't keep his ___ to Leigh.

____ 16. QUESTIONS   P. He asks Leigh to help with the flag at school.

____ 17. WRITER   Q. Mr. Henshaw moves to this state that has moose.

____ 18. MONSTERS   R. Most of the boys wrote about these.

____ 19. ALASKA   S. Friend from school who eats dinner with Leigh

____ 20. BARRY   T. Leigh's teacher

MATCHING 4
Dear Mr. Henshaw

____ 1. ALASKA   A. Leigh first writes about a ten-foot ___ man.

____ 2. BOTTS   B. Fictitious name on Leigh's lunch

____ 3. CANAPES   C. Bonnie's catering boss

____ 4. SHOES   D. Christmas present from Dad

____ 5. WAX   E. Mom, Dad, and Leigh made up silly songs about these.

____ 6. BUTTERFLY   F. Most of the boys wrote about these.

____ 7. RAIN   G. Last name of Leigh, Bonnie, and Bill

____ 8. MONSTERS   H. Having to answer these made Leigh mad at first.

____ 9. HENSHAW   I. Special little food items for Leigh's lunch

____ 10. GARBAGE   J. Author of Ways to Amuse a Dog

____ 11. JOE   K. It signals a low point or troubling time in the story.

____ 12. JACKET   L. Leigh visits the ___ trees.

____ 13. BARRY   M. Mr. Fridley gave Leigh the idea for this.

____ 14. BADGER   N. The refinery there shut down.

____ 15. SPRECKELS   O. Mr. Fridley sometimes guards this.

____ 16. QUESTIONS   P. She is the Famous Author the kids met for lunch.

____ 17. ALARM   Q. Leigh wants to be this when he grows up.

____ 18. WRITER   R. Mr. Henshaw moves to this state that has moose.

____ 19. KATY   S. Friend from school who eats dinner with Leigh

____ 20. FRIDLEY   T. He asks Leigh to help with the flag at school.

MATCHING 5
Dear Mr. Henshaw

____ 1. WAX   A. Mr. Fridley sometimes guards this.

____ 2. QUESTIONS   B. The refinery there shut down.

____ 3. PROMISES   C. Fictitious name on Leigh's lunch

____ 4. LEIGH   D. He is the protagonist, the main character in the story.

____ 5. MONSTERS   E. Most of the boys wrote about these.

____ 6. SPRECKELS   F. Friend from school who eats dinner with Leigh

____ 7. WRITER   G. She is the Famous Author the kids met for lunch.

____ 8. BUTTERFLY   H. Dad doesn't keep his ___ to Leigh.

____ 9. JOE   I. Mom, Dad, and Leigh made up silly songs about these.

____ 10. SHOES   J. Leigh visits the ___ trees.

____ 11. FRIDLEY   K. Nickname for Leigh's dad's truck

____ 12. LIBRARIAN   L. Setting for Beggar Bears

____ 13. BARRY   M. Last name of Leigh, Bonnie, and Bill

____ 14. GARBAGE   N. Leigh wants to be this when he grows up.

____ 15. MARTINEZ   O. She saved Mr. Henshaw's new book for Leigh.

____ 16. BADGER   P. Leigh's teacher

____ 17. BOTTS   Q. Leigh first writes about a ten-foot ___ man.

____ 18. YELLOWSTONE   R. He asks Leigh to help with the flag at school.

____ 19. RAIN   S. It signals a low point or troubling time in the story.

____ 20. RIG   T. Having to answer these made Leigh mad at first

MATCHING ANSWER KEYS
Dear Mr. Henshaw

	1	2	3	4	5
1	T	S	N	R	Q
2	I	C	B	G	T
3	C	L	P	I	H
4	H	B	I	E	D
5	R	T	G	A	E
6	A	K	F	L	B
7	Q	F	K	K	N
8	S	G	L	F	J
9	N	H	M	J	C
10	K	Q	C	O	I
11	E	M	D	B	R
12	M	D	A	D	O
13	O	J	O	S	F
14	G	R	J	P	A
15	L	I	T	N	P
16	D	A	E	H	G
17	J	E	H	M	M
18	B	O	R	Q	L
19	F	N	Q	C	S
20	P	P	S	T	K

FILL IN THE BLANKS 1
Dear Mr. Henshaw

_____ 1. Mr. Fridley gave Leigh the idea for this.

_____ 2. Last name of Leigh, Bonnie, and Bill

_____ 3. Setting for Beggar Bears

_____ 4. She is the Famous Author the kids met for lunch.

_____ 5. It signals a low point or troubling time in the story.

_____ 6. Leigh first writes about a ten-foot ___ man.

_____ 7. Nickname for Leigh's dad's truck

_____ 8. Fictitious name on Leigh's lunch

_____ 9. She saved Mr. Henshaw's new book for Leigh.

_____ 10. He is the protagonist, the main character in the story.

_____ 11. State where Leigh and his mom live

_____ 12. Author of Dear Mr. Henshaw

_____ 13. Leigh wants to be this when he grows up.

_____ 14. Dad doesn't keep his ___ to Leigh.

_____ 15. He asks Leigh to help with the flag at school.

FILL IN THE BLANKS 2
Dear Mr. Henshaw

_____ 1. State where Leigh and his mom live

_____ 2. Mr. Henshaw moves to this state that has moose.

_____ 3. Leigh visits the ___ trees.

_____ 4. Bonnie's catering boss

_____ 5. She saved Mr. Henshaw's new book for Leigh.

_____ 6. Having to answer these made Leigh mad at first.

_____ 7. She is the Famous Author the kids met for lunch.

_____ 8. Author of Dear Mr. Henshaw

_____ 9. Leigh's dog

_____ 10. Dad doesn't keep his ___ to Leigh.

_____ 11. The refinery there shut down.

_____ 12. Special book Leigh writes in

_____ 13. It signals a low point or troubling time in the story.

_____ 14. Friend from school who eats dinner with Leigh

_____ 15. I wonder if Dad will marry the ___ boy and his mother.

FILL IN THE BLANKS 3
Dear Mr. Henshaw

_____ 1. Author of Ways to Amuse a Dog

_____ 2. Christmas present from Dad

_____ 3. It signals a low point or troubling time in the story.

_____ 4. Fictitious name on Leigh's lunch

_____ 5. Mr. Henshaw moves to this state that has moose.

_____ 6. Leigh's teacher

_____ 7. The refinery there shut down.

_____ 8. I wonder if Dad will marry the ___ boy and his mother.

_____ 9. Most of the boys wrote about these.

_____ 10. Leigh first writes about a ten-foot ___ man.

_____ 11. He is the protagonist, the main character in the story.

_____ 12. Mr. Fridley sometimes guards this.

_____ 13. Bonnie's catering boss

_____ 14. He asks Leigh to help with the flag at school.

_____ 15. Special book Leigh writes in

FILL IN THE BLANKS 4
Dear Mr. Henshaw

_____ 1. Bonnie's catering boss

_____ 2. Leigh wants to be this when he grows up.

_____ 3. Author of Dear Mr. Henshaw

_____ 4. Leigh first writes about a ten-foot ___ man.

_____ 5. Setting for Beggar Bears

_____ 6. Leigh's teacher

_____ 7. Christmas present from Dad

_____ 8. Special book Leigh writes in

_____ 9. He is the protagonist, the main character in the story.

_____ 10. State where Leigh and his mom live

_____ 11. It signals a low point or troubling time in the story.

_____ 12. Mom, Dad, and Leigh made up silly songs about these.

_____ 13. Having to answer these made Leigh mad at first.

_____ 14. Mr. Henshaw moves to this state that has moose.

_____ 15. Friend from school who eats dinner with Leigh

FILL IN THE BLANKS 5
Dear Mr. Henshaw

_____ 1. Having to answer these made Leigh mad at first.

_____ 2. Friend from school who eats dinner with Leigh

_____ 3. Most of the boys wrote about these.

_____ 4. It signals a low point or troubling time in the story.

_____ 5. Bonnie's catering boss

_____ 6. She saved Mr. Henshaw's new book for Leigh.

_____ 7. Nickname for Leigh's dad's truck

_____ 8. Last name of Leigh, Bonnie, and Bill

_____ 9. Mom, Dad, and Leigh made up silly songs about these.

_____ 10. I wonder if Dad will marry the ___ boy and his mother.

_____ 11. Setting for Beggar Bears

_____ 12. Leigh visits the ___ trees.

_____ 13. He asks Leigh to help with the flag at school.

_____ 14. Leigh's teacher

_____ 15. Christmas present from Dad

FILL IN THE BLANKS ANSWER KEYS
Dear Mr. Henshaw

	1	2	3	4	5
1	ALARM	CALIFORNIA	HENSHAW	KATY	QUESTIONS
2	BOTTS	ALASKA	JACKET	WRITER	BARRY
3	YELLOWSTONE	BUTTERFLY	RAIN	CLEARY	MONSTERS
4	BADGER	KATY	JOE	WAX	RAIN
5	RAIN	LIBRARIAN	ALASKA	YELLOWSTONE	KATY
6	WAX	QUESTIONS	MARTINEZ	MARTINEZ	LIBRARIAN
7	RIG	BADGER	SPRECKELS	JACKET	RIG
8	JOE	CLEARY	PIZZA	DIARY	BOTTS
9	LIBRARIAN	BANDIT	MONSTERS	LEIGH	SHOES
10	LEIGH	PROMISES	WAX	CALIFORNIA	PIZZA
11	CALIFORNIA	SPRECKELS	LEIGH	RAIN	YELLOWSTONE
12	CLEARY	DIARY	GARBAGE	SHOES	BUTTERFLY
13	WRITER	RAIN	KATY	QUESTIONS	FRIDLEY
14	PROMISES	BARRY	FRIDLEY	ALASKA	MARTINEZ
15	FRIDLEY	PIZZA	DIARY	BARRY	JACKET

SHORT ANSWER 1
Dear Mr. Henshaw
Answer fully in complete sentences.

1. Why does Leigh's mom feel that Leigh should answer the list of questions that Mr. Henshaw sent him?

2. What does Leigh's dad do for a living? Why was that a problem for Leigh and his mother?

3. Leigh has a problem with his lunch. What is it? How does Leigh feel about this? Why?

4. How does Mr. Fridley help Leigh?

5. How does Leigh feel when his father doesn't call?

6. What happens to Bandit while he is traveling with Leigh's father in the rig?

7. What does Leigh's mom mean when she says Leigh's dad will never grow up?

8. How does Leigh's burglar alarm change things for Leigh at school?

9. What concern does Leigh have about inviting Barry to visit?

10. How does Mrs. Badger describe Mr. Henshaw?

SHORT ANSWER 1 ANSWER KEY
Dear Mr. Henshaw

1. Why does Leigh's mom feel that Leigh should answer the list of questions that Mr. Henshaw sent him?
    She feels that if Mr. Henshaw took the time to answer Leigh's questions from his letter, Leigh should take the time to answer Mr. Henshaw's questions.

2. What does Leigh's dad do for a living? Why was that a problem for Leigh and his mother?
    Leigh's dad drives a truck around central California. Leigh and his mother didn't like it because he was gone too much.

3. Leigh has a problem with his lunch. What is it? How does Leigh feel about this? Why?
    Leigh's problem is that people keep stealing the good things out of his lunch. He is very upset by this because his mom puts special things in his lunch. The best parts get taken.

4. How does Mr. Fridley help Leigh?
    Mr. Fridley pays attention to Leigh, which makes him feel more important and not so "medium." Mr. Fridley is the one who gives Leigh the idea of putting a burglar alarm on his lunch so it would not keep getting stolen.

5. How does Leigh feel when his father doesn't call?
    Leigh feels sad, lonely, hurt, and disappointed.

6. What happens to Bandit while he is traveling with Leigh's father in the rig?
    Bandit jumps out of the truck in a snow storm and does not come back to the truck. The road is about to close, and Leigh's father has to leave, so Bandit is left behind.

7. What does Leigh's mom mean when she says Leigh's dad will never grow up?
    She means that Leigh's father will never change. He will never learn to take responsibility for anything other than his truck.

8. How does Leigh's burglar alarm change things for Leigh at school?
    He gets positive attention from the other students and even from the principal due to his invention. He starts to feel that he is not so "medium" after all.

9. What concern does Leigh have about inviting Barry to visit?
    He is afraid that Barry will not like his house because it is so much smaller than Barry's and because there is mildew in the bathroom.

10. How does Mrs. Badger describe Mr. Henshaw?
    She describes him as "a very nice young man with a wicked twinkle in his eye."

SHORT ANSWER 2
Dear Mr. Henshaw
Answer fully in complete sentences.

1. Why does Leigh read *Ways to Amuse a Dog* so many times?

2. What finally convinces Leigh to write the answers to Mr. Henshaw's questions?

3. What are some of the things that bother Leigh?

4. Why is Leigh rude to Mr. Henshaw in his letter?

5. What are some of the ways that Leigh tries to keep people from stealing his lunch?

Dear Mr. Henshaw Short Answer 2 Page 2

6. The librarian stops Leigh in the hall and asks him to come to the library. Why?

7. According to Leigh's mom, a trucker's life is not easy. Why?

8. Leigh leaves his classroom with someone else's lunchbag. What is he going to do with it? What happens to stop him?

9. Why is Leigh glad that he didn't catch the "lunchbox thief"?

10. How does Leigh feel when Mrs. Badger calls him an author?

SHORT ANSWER 2 ANSWER KEY
Dear Mr. Henshaw

1. Why does Leigh read Ways to Amuse a Dog so many times?
    His teacher reads it aloud to the class, and Leigh thinks it is funny. Also it is about a dog, which reminded him of his dog Bandit.

2. What finally convinces Leigh to write the answers to Mr. Henshaw's questions?
    Leigh's mom says that if he really wants to become an author, he needs to write more--and answering the questions is the best way to get started.

3. What are some of the things that bother Leigh?
    Leigh is bothered when someone steals something from his lunch bag, by having to walk to school slowly, by being left alone before school, by his father's not phoning, and by his father's calling him "kid."

4. Why is Leigh rude to Mr. Henshaw in his letter?
    Leigh's dad forgets to send the December support payment and does not come to see him. Leigh is angry about that and takes it out on Mr. Henshaw.

5. What are some of the ways that Leigh tries to keep people from stealing his lunch?
    Leigh tries to keep people from stealing his lunch by eating it on the way to school, putting a fictitious name on the lunchbag, and watching who goes behind the partition where the lunches are kept.

6. The librarian stops Leigh in the hall and asks him to come to the library. Why?
    The librarian has Mr. Henshaw's new book and tells Leigh he can be the first one to read it. She says that she knows he loves books by Mr. Henshaw because he checks them out so often.

7. According to Leigh's mom, a trucker's life is not easy. Why?
    Truckers sometimes lose some of their heariing in their left ear from the wind rushing past the driver's window. Truckers also get out of shape from sitting such long hours without exercise and from eating too much greasy food. Sometimes they get ulcers from the strain of trying to make good time on the highway.

8. Leigh leaves his classroom with someone else's lunchbag. What is he going to do with it? What happens to stop him?
    Leigh is ready to kick the lunch down the hallway when Mr. Fridley sees him. Mr. Fridley tells Leigh he does not want a nice boy like him to get into trouble and that if he wants friends, he needs to stop scowling. He tells Leigh lots of kids have problems and to figure out how to handle his problems better.

Dear Mr. Henshaw Short Answer 2 Answer Key Page 2

9. Why is Leigh glad that he didn't catch the "lunchbox thief"?
    He is glad he didn't catch the "lunchbox thief" because if the thief had set off the alarm in the classroom, the thief would have been in big trouble, and Leigh didn't want to get anyone in trouble since he had to go to school with whomever it was. He just wanted his lunch every day.

10. How does Leigh feel when Mrs. Badger calls him an author?
    He is a little embarrassed, but he is very proud.

SHORT ANSWER 3
Dear Mr. Henshaw
Answer fully in complete sentences.

1. What format does Beverly Cleary use in her book? How does this affect the story?

2. In the beginning of the book, is Leigh a popular boy with the other students in his new school? How do you know this?

3. What are some of the ways that Leigh tries to keep people from stealing his lunch?

4. How does Mr. Fridley help Leigh?

5. The librarian stops Leigh in the hall and asks him to come to the library. Why?

Dear Mr. Henshaw Short Answer 3 Page 2

6. What happens to Bandit while he is traveling with Leigh's father in the rig?

7. Why is Leigh upset about the sugar refinery shutting down near his home?

8. Leigh leaves his classroom with someone else's lunchbag. What is he going to do with it? What happens to stop him?

9. How does Leigh feel about his burglar alarm invention?

10. How does Mrs. Badger describe Mr. Henshaw?

SHORT ANSWER 3 ANSWER KEY
Dear Mr. Henshaw

1. What format does Beverly Cleary use in her book? How does this affect the story?
    Beverly Cleary uses the format of a series of letters and diary entries. The readers get everything from Leigh's point of view, which gives us insights into his life and thinking as well as drawing us closer to him as a character.

2. In the beginning of the book, is Leigh a popular boy with the other students in his new school? How do you know this?
    Answers should reflect that he is not popular with the other students. Here are some examples of how we know this: someone steals the best parts of his lunch, he says the kids at school are more interested in his lunch than in him, he stays after school to kick the ball around but no one plays with him.

3. What are some of the ways that Leigh tries to keep people from stealing his lunch?
    Leigh tries to keep people from stealing his lunch by eating it on the way to school, putting a fictitious name on the lunchbag, and watching who goes behind the partition where the lunches are kept.

4. How does Mr. Fridley help Leigh?
    Mr. Fridley pays attention to Leigh, which makes him feel more important and not so "medium." Mr. Fridley is the one who gives Leigh the idea of putting a burglar alarm on his lunch so it would not keep getting stolen.

5. The librarian stops Leigh in the hall and asks him to come to the library. Why?
    The librarian has Mr. Henshaw's new book and tells Leigh he can be the first one to read it. She says that she knows he loves books by Mr. Henshaw because he checks them out so often.

6. What happens to Bandit while he is traveling with Leigh's father in the rig?
    Bandit jumps out of the truck in a snow storm and does not come back to the truck. The road is about to close, and Leigh's father has to leave, so Bandit is left behind.

7. Why is Leigh upset about the sugar refinery shutting down near his home?
    Leigh is afraid he will never see his father again if the refinery shuts down giving his father no work-related reason to come to the area.

Dear Mr. Henshaw Short Answer 3 Answer Key Page 2

8. Leigh leaves his classroom with someone else's lunchbag. What is he going to do with it? What happens to stop him?
> Leigh is ready to kick the lunch down the hallway when Mr. Fridley sees him. Mr. Fridley tells Leigh he does not want a nice boy like him to get into trouble and that if he wants friends, he needs to stop scowling. He tells Leigh lots of kids have problems and to figure out how to handle his problems better.

9. How does Leigh feel about his burglar alarm invention?
> He is excited and proud that the invention worked, and he is excited that others liked, and some even copied, his invention.

10. How does Mrs. Badger describe Mr. Henshaw?
> She describes him as "a very nice young man with a wicked twinkle in his eye."

EXTENDED ANSWERS 1
Dear Mr. Henshaw

Answer these questions thoroughly using complete paragraphs. Use the back of this page or an additional page if you do not have room enough to express your answer in the space provided.

1. Why does Mr. Henshaw keep answering Leigh's letters, even though he is very busy?

2. Describe Leigh's relationship with his father. Give a complete answer, and support your statements with evidence from the book.

3. What are the main conflicts in Dear Mr. Henshaw? State and briefly explain each.

EXTENDED ANSWERS 2
Dear Mr. Henshaw

Answer these questions thoroughly using complete paragraphs. Use the back of this page or an additional page if you do not have room enough to express your answer in the space provided.

1. Persuade me that Mr. Henshaw actually changed Leigh's life.

2. How did Leigh's parents divorce affect him?

3. Explain how Dear Mr. Henshaw is a story about relationships.

EXTENDED ANSWERS 3
Dear Mr. Henshaw

Answer these questions thoroughly using complete paragraphs. Use the back of this page or an additional page if you do not have room enough to express your answer in the space provided.

1. Leigh was lonely at the beginning of the book. Why? Also explain how you think he feels at the end of the story and why.

2. Several people help Leigh. Name at least three people who helped him in the book. Explain how and why each person helped him using evidence from the book and your own personal experiences.

3. Why is the burglar alarm such a big deal in the book? What is the result of Leigh's successfully creating the alarm?

QUOTATIONS 1
Dear Mr. Henshaw

Explain the significance of these quotations. Use the back of this page or an additional page if you do not have room enough to express your answers in the spaces provided.

1. "Your father isn't a bad man by any means."

2. She called me an author. *A real live author called me an author.*

3. Dad's stomach hung over his belt, and he wasn't as tall as I remembered him.

4. Dad, you keep Bandit. You need him more than I do. ... Please take him. I don't have any way to amuse him.

QUOTATIONS 2
Dear Mr. Henshaw

Explain the significance of these quotations. Use the back of this page or an additional page if you do not have room enough to express your answers in the spaces provided.

1. Dear Mr. Henshaw, I am the boy who wrote to you last year when I was in the second grade.

2. Well, keep your nose clean, kid.

3. Most truckers ate real fast and left, but Dad kidded around for a while and played the video games.

4. Maybe you don't [care], but I do.

QUOTATIONS 3
Dear Mr. Henshaw

Explain the significance of these quotations. Use the back of this page or an additional page if you do not have room enough to express your answers in the spaces provided.

1. Hey, Bill, Mom wants to know when we're going out to get the pizza?

2. Sorry about Bandit. Here's $20. Go buy yourself an ice cream cone.

3. I began to feel like some sort of hero. Maybe I'm not so medium after all.

4. Don't think you are the only boy around here with a father who forgets.

QUOTATIONS 4
Dear Mr. Henshaw

Explain the significance of these quotations. Use the back of this page or an additional page if you do not have room enough to express your answers in the spaces provided.

1. Bandit and I didn't get a divorce. They did.

2. The man is made of wax, and every time he crosses the desert, he melts a little.

3. I can't hate him. Maybe things would be easier if I could.

4. The California bear was right side up so maybe Mr. Fridley didn't need me to help him after all.

MULTIPLE CHOICE 1
Dear Mr. Henshaw

1. Why does Leigh read Ways to Amuse a Dog so many times?
    A. Leigh is trying to memorize the book, so he reads it over and over again.
    B. Ways to Amuse a Dog is the only book he owns, and he likes to read, so he reads it over and over again.
    C. He reads it because his teacher read it aloud to them in class, and Leigh thought it was funny. Also it is about a dog which reminds him of his dog Bandit.
    D. He is afraid he'll lose the book, and he wants to remember the story forever, to be able to tell it to his kids someday.

2. What finally convinces Leigh to write the answers to Mr. Henshaw's questions?
    A. Leigh's dad tells him to do it.
    B. Leigh wants to find out more about writing, and he thinks Mr. Henshaw is his best source, so he decides to answer the questions in hopes of getting more information later.
    C. Leigh gets tired of trying to decide whether to write or not to write, so he just goes ahead and does it.
    D. Leigh's mom says that if he really wants to become an author, he needs to write more, and answering the questions is the best way to get started.

3. Which is NOT something that bothers Leigh?
    A. Leigh is bothered when someone steals something from his lunch bag.
    B. Leigh is bothered by being left alone before school.
    C. Leigh is bothered by his father's calling him "kid."
    D. Leigh is bothered by having "catering" food packed as his lunch.

4. Who gives Leigh the idea to start writing in a diary?
    A. His mom
    B. Mr. Henshaw
    C. Mr. Firdley
    D. Miss Neely

5. Leigh has a problem with his lunch. What is it?
    A. The problem is that he keeps forgetting his lunch.
    B. The problem is that his lunch gets squished in the classroom coat closet.
    C. The problem is that people keep stealing the good things out of his lunch.
    D. The problem is that his mom packs the same, boring peanut butter sandwich every day.

Dear Mr. Henshaw Multiple Choice 1 Page 2

6. According to Leigh's teacher, his writing skills are improving. Why?
    A. He is being tutored after school.
    B. His mother is helping him learn to write better.
    C. He is reading and writing a lot.
    D. He is writing a lot of letters to his dad.

7. Why is Leigh upset about the sugar refinery shutting down near his home?
    A. His mother will be unemployed, and they will have an even more difficult time making ends meet.
    B. He is afraid that his father will not need to pick up loads of sugar anymore, and he may never see his dad again.
    C. He knows a lot of people depend on the refinery for their living, and he feels sorry for the people who will lose their jobs.
    D. He thinks when the sugar refinery shuts down, his father will be unemployed and won't be able to send him gifts anymore.

8. What does Leigh's mom mean when she says Leigh's dad will never grow up?
    A. She means Leigh's father will never stop throwing temper tantrums and demanding his own way.
    B. She means that Leigh's father will never learn to take responsiblity for anything other than his truck.
    C. She means Leigh's father will always see things in a simple way.
    D. She means Leigh's father will always have a wonderful, childish sense of humor.

9. Why is Leigh glad that he doesn't catch the lunchbox thief?
    A. Catching the thief could have been embarrassing.
    B. He doesn't want to get anyone in trouble because he would have to live with that person for the rest of the school year.
    C. The identity of the thief will always be an unsolved mystery, something fun to think and laugh about for years to come.
    D. He secretly enjoys the daily drama of wondering who the thief is.

10. Why does Leigh say he hates his father?
    A. Leigh gets mad because his dad won't take him along on the rig, so he says he hates his father out of anger.
    B. Leigh says he hates his father to try to make his mother feel better.
    C. Leigh hates that his father is not more like Mr. Henshaw.
    D. Leigh's father often does not keep his promises to Leigh. That hurts Leigh, so he says he hates his father.

MULTIPLE CHOICE 2
Dear Mr. Henshaw

1. What does Mr. Henshaw tell Leigh to do in order to be an author?
    A. Leigh should interview other authors.
    B. Leigh should wait until he grows up a little more.
    C. Leigh should buy a computer.
    D. Leigh should read a different book that Mr. Henshaw wrote.

2. What is the point of view of this section of the book?
    A. It is written in first person point of view.
    B. It is written from the omniscient point of view.
    C. It is written from the third person point of view.
    D. It is written from the second person point of view.

3. Which of the following sentences does NOT mean that Leigh was not popular at school?
    A. "I'm just a boy nobody pays much attention to."
    B. "The kids here pay more attention to my lunch than they do to me."
    C. "A new boy in school has to be pretty cautious until he gets to know who's who."
    D. "I don't have a whole lot of friends in my new school"

4. Why is Leigh rude to Mr. Henshaw in his letter?
    A. Leigh is rude to Mr. Henshaw because his dad forgot to send the December support payment and because his dad does not come to see him.
    B. Leigh is rude to Mr. Henshaw because his mom wanted him to stop writing, but he didn't want to stop.
    C. Leigh is rude to Mr. Henshaw because Mr. Henshaw sent him even more questions.
    D. Leigh is rude to Mr. Henshaw because he is mad at his mom, and he got a bad grade on his book report.

5. Which of the following is NOT a way that Leigh tries to keep people from stealing his lunch?
    A. Leigh keeps watch to see who goes near the lunches.
    B. Leigh puts a fictitious name on his lunchbag.
    C. Leigh eats his lunch on the way to school.
    D. Leigh keeps his lunch in his desk.

Dear Mr. Henshaw Multiple Choice 2 Page 2

6. What happens to Bandit while he is traveling with Leigh's father in his rig?
    A. Leigh's father gives him to another trucker who is lonely.
    B. He gets stolen.
    C. He is hit by another truck.
    D. He jumps out of the truck and does not come back.

7. Which of the statements below is NOT a reason a trucker's life is not easy, according to Leigh's mom?
    A. Truckers are stuck between the shipper of the goods and the customer; they have to try to keep people on both ends of the sale happy.
    B. Truckers sometimes lose some of their hearing in their left ear from the wind rushing past the driver's window.
    C. Truckers get out of shape from sitting such long hours without exercise and from eating too much greasy food.
    D. Sometimes truckers get ulcers from the strain of trying to make good time.

8. What does Leigh's mom mean when she says Leigh's dad will never grow up?
    A. She means Leigh's father will always have a wonderful, childish sense of humor.
    B. She means Leigh's father will always see things in a simple way.
    C. She means Leigh's father will never stop throwing temper tantrums and demanding his own way.
    D. She means that Leigh's father will never learn to take responsibility for anything other than his truck.

9. Does Leigh's burglar alarm change things for him at school?
    A. Yes, other students become jealous of his invention and give him an even harder time than before.
    B. Yes, Leigh gets sent to the principal's office for making such a noise in class.
    C. Yes, Leigh gets more positive attention and starts to feel that he is not so "medium" after all.
    D. No, nothing changes. The burglar alarm seemed like a good idea, but it didn't work.

10. What does Mrs. Badger like best about "A Day on Dad's Rig"?
    A. Mrs. Badger likes that Leigh wrote about something that was fictional and made completely from his own imagination.
    B. Mrs. Badger likes that his spelling and punctuation are correct and his handwriting is neat.
    C. Mrs. Badger likes that "it was written by a boy who wrote honestly about something he knew and had strong feelings about."
    D. Mrs. Badger likes the part about the peak from which Black Bart's lookout used to signal to Black Bart to rob the people coming through the pass.

MULTIPLE CHOICE 3
Dear Mr. Henshaw

1. Leigh's mom is very busy. What are some of the things that she does?
    A. She takes care of Leigh, works as a caterer, and goes to the community college.
    B. She works in an office, takes care of Leigh, and goes to the community college.
    C. She works as a caterer, takes care of Leigh, and occasionally goes on the road with Leigh's dad.
    D. She is a professional writer who also teaches at the community college.

2. Why does Mr. Frindley want Leigh to come to school a few minutes early?
    A. Mr. Frindley wants Leigh to come early to hide his lunch.
    B. Mr. Frindley wants Leigh to help him put up the flag.
    C. Mr. Frindley tutors Leigh before school.
    D. Mr. Frindley wants Leigh to help clean the boards.

3. Leigh has trouble when he first starts to write in his diary. What does Mr. Henshaw suggest that helps him?
    A. Mr. Henshaw suggests that he should wait until something exciting happens and then write about that in his diary.
    B. Mr. Henshaw suggests that he should talk to his teacher or his mom about what to write.
    C. Mr. Henshaw suggests that he should play music while he is writing because that's what Mr. Henshaw does.
    D. Mr. Henshaw suggests that he should pretend that he is writing to someone.

4. The librarian stops Leigh in the hall and asks him to come to the library. Why?
    A. He has a book overdue, and she does not want him to forget about it.
    B. She wants to help Leigh find another author he would enjoy, other than Mr. Henshaw.
    C. She wants Leigh to be the first one to have Mr. Henshaw's new book.
    D. She has a new book by Angela Badger that she thinks he would enjoy.

5. How does Leigh feel when his father doesn't call?
    A. He feels sad, hurt, and disappointed.
    B. He feels worried that something has happened to his dad.
    C. He doesn't care.
    D. He feels relieved because his dad was mad at him.

6. Which of the following is NOT a reason Leigh's mom uses to explain why Leigh's dad loves trucking?
   A. He loves the excitement of never knowing where his next trip will take him.
   B. He loves the feel of power of controlling a mighty machine.
   C. He loves being away from home, out on the open road with no one to bother him.
   D. He loves the mountains and the desert sunrises and the sight of the orange trees heavy with oranges and the smell of fresh-mown alfalfa.

7. Leigh's mom used to ride with his dad in the truck on trips, but she says that she got tired of doing that. How does that make Leigh feel?
   A. It makes Leigh feel better because it means that she did not give up riding with his dad because he (Leigh) was born.
   B. It makes Leigh feel uneasy; he isn't used to his mother sharing this kind of information with him.
   C. It makes Leigh feel angry because by not putting her own desires aside, his mom was being as much of a child as his father was.
   D. It makes Leigh feel sad because he wants his mom to still enjoy riding with is dad.

8. Leigh leaves his classroom with someone else's lunchbag. What does he want to do with it?
   A. He wants to throw the bag into the trash.
   B. He wants to eat the whole lunch.
   C. He wants to drop kick the bag in the hallway.
   D. He wants to steal the best things out of the bag.

9. What does Leigh buy with the twenty dollars that his father sent him?
   A. Leigh buys things to make a "burgler alarm" for his lunch box.
   B. Leigh buys his mother a present with the twenty dollars.
   C. Leigh buys three books by Mr. Henshaw.
   D. Leigh buys writing supplies--a new notebook, some writing paper, pens, and pencils.

10. Why does Leigh give Bandit back to his father?
    A. Leigh gets used to not having Bandit at home.
    B. Leigh thinks having Bandit will make his father more responsible.
    C. Leigh has friends now and doesn't need Bandit.
    D. Leigh thinks his father needs Bandit more than he does.

MULTIPLE CHOICE ANSWER KEYS
Dear Mr. Henshaw

	1	2	3
1	C	D	A
2	D	A	B
3	D	C	D
4	B	A	C
5	C	D	A
6	C	D	C
7	B	A	A
8	B	D	C
9	B	C	A
10	D	C	D

VOCABULARY 1
Dear Mr. Henshaw

____ 1. autographed   A. Thankful

____ 2. according   B. Making a person feel ashamed or uncomfortable

____ 3. nagging   C. Ordinary sentences; without poetic form

____ 4. quilted   D. To act or do as another has acted or done

____ 5. mimeograph   E. Make copies using a typed stencil and ink, using a machine for that purpose

____ 6. scowling   F. Mixture of foods baked in a single dish

____ 7. wrath   G. A showing of something, as a process or how to

____ 8. reception   H. To scold, complain, or to constantly find fault

____ 9. villains   I. Strong anger

____ 10. grateful   J. Something that has person's own signature or handwriting

____ 11. demonstration   K. Ability to get a transmission or signal

____ 12. embarrassing   L. Wicked or evil people; scoundrels

____ 13. prose   M. Having a gloomy or unhappy facial expression

____ 14. casserole   N. To pad and stitch ornamentally or to stitch layers of fabric together

____ 15. imitate   O. As determined by or in keeping with

VOCABULARY 2
Dear Mr. Henshaw

____ 1. amuse

____ 2. hauling

____ 3. refinery

____ 4. nuisance

____ 5. comfortable

____ 6. desert

____ 7. wrath

____ 8. molest

____ 9. quivering

____ 10. villains

____ 11. insulated

____ 12. fastening

____ 13. prowls

____ 14. avoid

____ 15. splendid

A. Strong anger

B. A dry, often sandy region of little rainfall, extreme temperatures, and sparse vegetation

C. Evil characters; bad guys

D. An industrial plant for purifying a crude substance such as petroleum or sugar

E. Wonderful; excellent; great

F. Trembling; shaking

G. Walks stealthily, as if hunting

H. At ease; relaxed

I. To try to keep away from

J. Something or someone that is annoying

K. To transport as with a truck or cart

L. Coated; surrounded and isolated

M. To occupy in an agreeable, pleasing, or entertaining fashion

N. Attaching

O. Bother or interfere with

VOCABULARY 3
Dear Mr. Henshaw

____ 1. diorama   A. Part of a telephone

____ 2. barreling   B. Strange; bizarre; sometimes involving the supernatural

____ 3. rude   C. Belonging to, made in, or typical of an earlier period

____ 4. fictitious   D. Something that is made up in an author's imagination or is not real

____ 5. pseudonym   E. An author's pen-name

____ 6. decided   F. Make less noisy by covering

____ 7. hibernated   G. To move at a high speed

____ 8. ulcers   H. Came to a conclusion after thinking about something

____ 9. mildew   I. Skin or other tissue breaking down

____ 10. receiver   J. Ill-mannered; discourteous

____ 11. antique   K. To try to keep away from

____ 12. weird   L. A three-demensional scene in which figures, stuffed wildlife, or other objects are arranged naturalistically against a painted background

____ 13. muffle   M. A pattern of horizontal and vertical lines of different colors

____ 14. avoid   N. To be in an inactive state or period

____ 15. plaid   O. Any of various fungi that form a superficial, usually whitish growth on plants or other surfaces

VOCABULARY 4
Dear Mr. Henshaw

____ 1. amuse

____ 2. diorama

____ 3. nagging

____ 4. fictitious

____ 5. scowling

____ 6. comfortable

____ 7. reception

____ 8. antique

____ 9. quivering

____ 10. villains

____ 11. insulated

____ 12. prowls

____ 13. avoid

____ 14. prose

____ 15. splendid

A. Trembling; shaking

B. Ability to get a transmission or signal

C. A three-dimensional scene in which figures, stuffed wildlife, or other objects are arranged against a painted background

D. Wonderful; excellent; great

E. Coated; surrounded and isolated

F. Wicked or evil people; scoundrels

G. Ordinary sentences; without poetic form

H. To scold, complain, or to constantly find fault

I. To occupy in an agreeable, pleasing, or entertaining fashion

J. Belonging to, made in, or typical of an earlier period

K. Walks stealthily, as if hunting

L. To try to keep away from

M. Having a gloomy or unhappy facial expression

N. Something that is made up; not real

O. At ease; relaxed

VOCABULARY 5
Dear Mr. Henshaw

____ 1. nuisance   A. Coated; surrounded and isolated

____ 2. fictitious   B. Make less noisy by covering

____ 3. pseudonym   C. To act or do as another has acted or done

____ 4. decided   D. Strange; bizarre; sometimes involving the supernatural

____ 5. scowling   E. An author's pen-name

____ 6. comfortable   F. Came to a conclusion after thinking about something

____ 7. ulcers   G. A showing of something, as a process or how to

____ 8. wrath   H. At ease; relaxed

____ 9. receiver   I. Walks stealthily, as if hunting

____ 10. weird   J. Having a gloomy or unhappy facial expression

____ 11. insulated   K. Part of a telephone

____ 12. demonstration   L. Strong anger

____ 13. muffle   M. Something that is made up; not real

____ 14. prowls   N. Something or someone that is annoying

____ 15. imitate   O. Skin or other tissue breaking down

VOCABULARY ANSWER KEYS
Dear Mr. Henshaw

	1	2	3	4	5
1	J	M	L	I	N
2	O	K	G	C	M
3	H	D	J	H	E
4	N	J	D	N	F
5	E	H	E	M	J
6	M	B	H	O	H
7	I	A	N	B	O
8	K	O	I	J	L
9	L	F	O	A	K
10	A	C	A	F	D
11	G	L	C	E	A
12	B	N	B	K	G
13	C	G	F	L	B
14	F	I	K	G	I
15	D	E	M	D	C

SHORT ANSWER STUDY QUESTIONS
Dear Mr. Henshaw

Section One: May 12-November 16
1. Who is the main character of *Dear Mr. Henshaw*?
2. What does Mr. Henshaw tell Leigh to do in order to be an author?
3. Why does Leigh read *Ways to Amuse a Dog* so many times?
4. Why does Leigh's mom feel that Leigh should answer the list of questions that Mr. Henshaw sent him?
5. What format does Beverly Cleary use in her book?
6. What is the point of view of this section of the book? How do you know?

Section Two: November 20-December 1
1. What finally convinces Leigh to write the answers to Mr. Henshaw's questions?
2. Why does Leigh's dad take Bandit?
3. What does Leigh's dad do for a living? Why was that a problem for Leigh and his mother?
4. In the story, what is a "rig"?
5. Leigh's mom is very busy. What are some of the things that she does?
6. Why do Leigh and his mom move from Bakersfield to Pacific Grove, California?
7. In the beginning of the book, is Leigh a popular boy with the other students in his new school? Choose a sentence from the book to support your answer.
8. What are some of the things that bother Leigh?
9. What does Leigh's dad's truck look like?

Section Three: December 4-December 21
1. Why is Leigh rude to Mr. Henshaw in his letter?
2. Leigh has a problem with his lunch. What is it? How does Leigh feel about this? Why?
3. Leigh has trouble when he first starts to write in his diary. What does Mr. Henshaw suggest that helps him?

Section Four: December 22-December 25
1. What are some of the ways that Leigh tries to keep people from stealing his lunch?
2. Since Leigh's dad did not spend Christmas with them the first year after the divorce, how does Leigh get his present, and what is it?

Section Five: January 3-January 10
1. What physical characteristic does Leigh share with his father?
2. What things are stolen from Leigh's lunch box?
3. How does Mr. Fridley help Leigh?

Section Six: January 12-January 19
1. The librarian stops Leigh in the hall and asks him to come to the library. Why?
2. According to Leigh's teacher, his writing skills are improving. Why do you think that is?

Dear Mr. Henshaw Study Questions Page 2

Section Seven: January 20-February 4
1. How does Leigh feel when his father doesn't call?
2. What happens to Bandit while he is traveling with Leigh's father in the rig?
3. According to Leigh's mom, a trucker's life is not easy. Why?
4. Why is Leigh upset about the sugar refinery shutting down near his home?
5. What does Leigh's mom think is the reason that Leigh's dad loves trucking?

Section Eight: February 5
1. What does Leigh's mom mean when she says Leigh's dad will never grow up?
2. Leigh's mom used to ride with his dad in the truck on trips, but she says that she got tired of doing that. Why does that make Leigh feel better?

Section Nine: February 6-February 9
1. Leigh leaves his classroom with someone else's lunchbag. What is he going to do with it? What happens to stop him?
2. Why do you think Leigh is upset when his father sends him the twenty-dollar bill?

Section Ten: February 15-March 15
1. Why does Leigh get behind in his diary writing?
2. What does Leigh buy with the twenty dollars that his father sends him?
3. How does Leigh's burglar alarm change things for Leigh at school?
4. Why is Leigh glad that he didn't catch the "lunchbox thief"?
5. How does Leigh feel about his burglar alarm invention?

Section Eleven: March 16-March 24
1. What does Barry like about visiting Leigh's house?
2. What concern does Leigh have about inviting Barry to visit?

Section Twelve: March 25-March 31 (end of book)
1. Why does Leigh say he hates his father?
2. What does Mrs. Badger like best about "A Day on Dad's Rig"?
3. Why was Leigh often lonely?
4. What does Leigh's story win in the Young Writer's Contest?
5. Who is Angela Badger?
6. How does Mrs. Badger describe Mr. Henshaw?
7. How does Leigh feel when Mrs. Badger calls him an author?
8. How does Leigh's dad find Bandit?
9. Why does Leigh give Bandit back to his father?
10. Who are the main characters in *Dear Mr. Henshaw*?

MULTIPLE CHOICE QUESTIONS 1
Dear Mr. Henshaw

Section One: May 12-November 16

1. Who is the main character in *Dear Mr. Henshaw*?
    - A. Mr. Henshaw
    - B. Leigh's dad
    - C. Leigh Botts
    - D. Bandit
2. What does Mr. Henshaw tell Leigh to do in order to be an author?
    - A. Leigh should interview other authors.
    - B. Leigh should buy a computer.
    - C. Leigh should read a different book that Mr. Henshaw wrote.
    - D. Leigh should wait until he grows up a little more.
3. Why does Leigh read *Ways to Amuse a Dog* so many times?
    - A. He is afraid he'll lose the book, and he wants to remember the story forever, to be able to tell it to his kids someday.
    - B. *Ways to Amuse a Dog* is the only book he owns, and he likes to read, so he reads it over and over again.
    - C. Leigh is trying to memorize the book, so he reads it over and over again.
    - D. He reads it because his teacher read it aloud to them in class, and Leigh thought it was funny. Also it is about a dog which reminds him of his dog, Bandit.
4. Why does Leigh's mom feel that Leigh should answer the list of questions that Mr. Henshaw sent him?
    - A. She feels that since Mr. Henshaw took the time to answer his questions from his letter, Leigh should take the time to answer Mr. Henshaw's questions.
    - B. She feels that writing the answers is a good punishment for nagging Mr. Henshaw.
    - C. She likes Mr. Henshaw.
    - D. She is tired of Leigh nagging her, so she tells him to write back to Mr. Henshaw to keep him busy for a while.
5. What format does Beverly Cleary use in her book?
    - A. She uses the format of a series of letters.
    - B. She uses a typical novel format.
    - C. She uses the literary format.
    - D. She uses the format of a narrative.
6. What is the point of view of this section of the book?
    - A. It is written from the third person point of view.
    - B. It is written from the second person point of view.
    - C. It is written from the omniscient point of view.
    - D. It is written from the first person point of view.

MULTIPLE CHOICE QUESTIONS 2
Dear Mr. Henshaw

Section Two: November 20-December 1

1. What finally convinces Leigh to write the answers to Mr. Henshaw's questions?
    A. Leigh wants to find out more about writing, and he thinks Mr. Henshaw is his best source, so he decides to answer the questions in hopes of getting more information later.
    B. Leigh's dad tells him to do it.
    C. Leigh gets tired of trying to decide whether to write or not to write, so he just goes ahead and does it.
    D. Leigh's mom says that if he really wants to become an author, he needs to write more, and answering the questions is the best way to get started.

2. Which of the following is NOT a reason Leigh's dad takes Bandit on the road with him?
    A. He takes Bandit as a punishment to Leigh for not answering Mr. Henshaw's questions.
    B. Bandit likes going because he gets bored staying alone at home.
    C. Bandit helps Leigh's dad stay awake on long hauls.
    D. Leigh's mom says she cannot work and take care of Bandit.

3. What does Leigh's dad do for a living?
    A. He is a construction worker.
    B. He works for the animal control department driving a truck picking up stray animals.
    C. He is a truck driver.
    D. He is a writer.

4. In the story, what is a "rig"?
    A. A rig is fishing tackle.
    B. A rig is a truck.
    C. A rig is a set of events.
    D. A rig is an unfair advantage.

5. Leigh's mom is very busy. What are some of the things that she does?
    A. She works in an office, takes care of Leigh, and goes to the community college.
    B. She takes care of Leigh, works as a caterer, and goes to the community college.
    C. She is a professional writer who also teaches at the community college.
    D. She works as a caterer, takes care of Leigh, and occasionally goes on the road with Leigh's dad.

6. Why do Leigh and his mom move from Bakersfield to Pacific Grove, California?
    A. Leigh's dad is transferred to Pacific Grove.
    B. The schools are better in Pacific Grove.
    C. They want to live near Leigh's grandparents.
    D. Leigh's parents got divorced, and his mom wants to live near the ocean.

Dear Mr. Henshaw Multiple Choice Questions Section Two Page 2

7. Which of the following sentences does NOT mean that Leigh was not popular at school?
    A. "A new boy in school has to be pretty cautious until he gets to know who's who."
    B. "I'm just a boy nobody pays much attention to."
    C. "I don't have a whole lot of friends in my new school"
    D. "The kids here pay more attention to my lunch than they do to me."
8. Which is NOT something that bothers Leigh?
    A. Leigh is bothered by being left alone before school.
    B. Leigh is bothered when someone steals something from his lunch bag.
    C. Leigh is bothered by his father's calling him "kid."
    D. Leigh is bothered by having "catering" food packed as his lunch.
9. What does Leigh's dad's truck look like?
    A. The truck is fire-engine red, has a train whistle horn, and has (what seems to be) a thousand lights.
    B. The truck is blue with gold and black letters carefully printed on the side of the cab saying, "BOTT'S TRUCKING."
    C. The truck has a large, square back with a lift on the back for loading and unloading things.
    D. The truck is big and has ten wheels, two in front and eight in back.

MULTIPLE CHOICE QUESTIONS 3
Dear Mr. Henshaw

Section Three: December 4-December 21

1. Why is Leigh rude to Mr. Henshaw in his letter?
    A. Leigh is rude to Mr. Henshaw because his mom wanted him to stop writing, but he didn't want to stop.
    B. Leigh is rude to Mr. Henshaw because Mr. Henshaw sent him even more questions.
    C. Leigh is rude to Mr. Henshaw because he is mad at his mom, and he got a bad grade on his book report.
    D. Leigh is rude to Mr. Henshaw because his dad forgot to send the December support payment and because his dad does not come to see him.

2. Who gives Leigh the idea to start writing in a diary?
    A. Miss Neely
    B. His mom
    C. Mr. Firdley
    D. Mr. Henshaw

3. Why does Mr. Frindley want Leigh to come to school a few minutes early?
    A. Mr. Frindley wants Leigh to come early to hide his lunch.
    B. Mr. Frindley tutors Leigh before school.
    C. Mr. Frindley wants Leigh to help clean the boards.
    D. Mr. Frindley wants Leigh to help him put up the flag.

4. Leigh has a problem with his lunch. What is it?
    A. The problem is that his mom packs the same, boring peanut butter sandwich every day.
    B. The problem is that someone keeps stealing the good things out of his lunch.
    C. The problem is that his lunch gets squished in the classroom coat closet.
    D. The problem is that he keeps forgetting his lunch.

5. Leigh has trouble when he first starts to write in his diary. What does Mr. Henshaw suggest that helps him?
    A. Mr. Henshaw suggests that he should wait until something exciting happens and then write about that in his diary.
    B. Mr. Henshaw suggests that he should play music while he is writing because that's what Mr. Henshaw does.
    C. Mr. Henshaw suggests that he should talk to his teacher or his mom about what to write.
    D. Mr. Henshaw suggests that he should pretend that he is writing to someone.

MULTIPLE CHOICE QUESTIONS 4 & 5
Dear Mr. Henshaw

Section Four: December 22-December 25

1. Which of the following is NOT a way that Leigh tries to keep people from stealing his lunch?
    A. Leigh puts a fictitious name on his lunchbag.
    B. Leigh keeps his lunch in his desk.
    C. Leigh keeps watch to see who goes near the lunches.
    D. Leigh eats his lunch on the way to school.
2. Since Leigh's dad does not spend Christmas with him the first year after the divorce, how does Leigh get his present?
    A. Leigh's dad has it delivered to Leigh's house via a fellow trucker.
    B. Leigh finds the present on the front porch.
    C. Leigh's father brings it to him but only stays a moment.
    D. Leigh's dad sends it in the mail.

Section Five: January 2- January 10

1. What physical characteristic do Leigh and his father share?
    A. They are tall.
    B. The have red hair.
    C. They have straight teeth.
    D. They have big hands.
2. Which of the following things is NOT stolen from Leigh's lunch box?
    A. stuffed mushrooms
    B. peanut butter sandwich
    C. wedding cake
    D. deviled eggs
3. How does Mr. Fridley help Leigh?
    A. He pays attention to Leigh and gives him the idea of putting a burglar alarm on his lunch.
    B. He suggests to Leigh that if he wants to be a writer, writing every day by keeping a diary might be a good idea.
    C. He brings Leigh the supplies for making the burglar alarm.
    D. He helps Leigh keep an eye on the lunches to try to catch the lunch thief.

MULTIPLE CHOICE QUESTIONS 6
Dear Mr. Henshaw

Section Six: January 12-January 19

1. The librarian stops Leigh in the hall and asks him to come to the library. Why?
    A. He has a book overdue, and she does not want him to forget about it.
    B. She wants Leigh to be the first one to have Mr. Henshaw's new book.
    C. She has a new book by Angela Badger that she thinks he would enjoy.
    D. She wants to help Leigh find another author he would enjoy, other than Mr. Henshaw.
2. According to Leigh's teacher, his writing skills are improving. Why?
    A. He is being tutored after school.
    B. He is writing a lot of letters to his dad.
    C. His mother is helping him learn to write better.
    D. He is reading and writing a lot.

MULTIPLE CHOICE QUESTIONS 7
Dear Mr. Henshaw

Section Seven: January 20-February 4

1. How does Leigh feel when his father doesn't call?
    A. He doesn't care.
    B. He feels worried that something has happened to his dad.
    C. He feels relieved because his dad was mad at him.
    D. He feels sad, hurt, and disappointed.
2. What happens to Bandit while he is traveling with Leigh's father in his rig?
    A. Leigh's father gives him to another trucker who is lonely.
    B. He is hit by another truck.
    C. He gets stolen.
    D. He jumps out of the truck and does not come back.
3. Which of the statements below is NOT a reason a trucker's life is not easy, according to Leigh's mom?
    A. Sometimes truckers get ulcers from the strain of trying to make good time on the highway.
    B. Truckers sometimes lose some of their hearing in their left ear from the wind rushing past the driver's window.
    C. Truckers get out of shape from sitting such long hours without exercise and from eating too much greasy food.
    D. Truckers are stuck between the shipper of the goods and the customer; they have to try to keep people on both ends of the sale happy.
4. Why is Leigh upset about the sugar refinery shutting down near his home?
    A. His mother will be unemployed, and they will have an even more difficult time making ends meet.
    B. He thinks when the sugar refinery shuts down, his father will be unemployed and won't be able to send him gifts anymore.
    C. He knows a lot of people depend on the refinery for their living, and he feels sorry for the people who will lose their jobs.
    D. He is afraid that his father will not need to pick up loads of sugar anymore, and he may never see his dad again.
5. Which of the following is NOT a reason Leigh's mom uses to explain why Leigh's dad loves trucking?
    A. He loves the excitement of never knowing where his next trip will take him.
    B. He loves being away from home, out on the open road with no one to bother him.
    C. He loves the mountains and the desert sunrises and the sight of the orange trees heavy with oranges and the smell of fresh-mown alfalfa.
    D. He loves the feel of power of controlling a mighty machine.

MULTIPLE CHOICE QUESTIONS 8 & 9
Dear Mr. Henshaw

Section Eight: February 5

1. What does Leigh's mom mean when she says Leigh's dad will never grow up?
    A. She means Leigh's father will always see things in a simple way.
    B. She means Leigh's father will always have a wonderful, childish sense of humor.
    C. She means that Leigh's father will never learn to take responsibility for anything other than his truck.
    D. She means Leigh's father will never stop throwing temper tantrums and demanding his own way.

2. Leigh's mom used to ride with his dad in the truck on trips, but she says that she got tired of doing that. How does that make Leigh feel?
    A. It makes Leigh feel better because it means that she did not give up riding with his dad because he (Leigh) was born.
    B. It makes Leigh feel angry because by not putting her own desires aside, his mom was being as much of a child as his father was.
    C. It makes Leigh feel sad because he wants his mom to still enjoy riding with is dad.
    D. It makes Leigh feel uneasy; he isn't used to his mother sharing this kind of information with him.

Section Nine: February 6-February 9

1. Leigh leaves his classroom with someone else's lunchbag. What does he want to do with it?
    A. He wants to steal the best things out of the bag.
    B. He wants to throw the bag into the trash.
    C. He wants to drop kick the bag in the hallway.
    D. He wants to eat the whole lunch.

2. Why is Leigh upset when his father sends him the twenty-dollar bill?
    A. He thinks his father isn't really sorry about losing Bandit and doesn't understand how important Bandit is to him.
    B. He thinks his father should have sent him way more money than that.
    C. He thinks his father should have bought him a new dog instead of sending money.
    D. He thinks his mother will not let him keep the money.

MULTIPLE CHOICE QUESTIONS 10
Dear Mr. Henshaw

Section Ten: February 15-March 15

1. Which is NOT a reason Leigh gets behind in his diary writing?
    A. He has to buy a new notebook because he filled up the first one.
    B. He is working on his story.
    C. He is writing to Mr. Henshaw.
    D. He spends too much time playing with Barry and his other classmates.

2. What does Leigh buy with the twenty dollars that his father sent him?
    A. Leigh buys writing supplies--a new notebook, some writing paper, pens, and pencils.
    B. Leigh buys his mother a present with the twenty dollars.
    C. Leigh buys things to make a "burgler alarm" for his lunch box.
    D. Leigh buys three books by Mr. Henshaw.

3. Does Leigh's burglar alarm change things for him at school?
    A. No, nothing changes. The burglar alarm seemed like a good idea, but it didn't really work.
    B. Yes, Leigh gets sent to the principal's office for making such a noise in class.
    C. Yes, Leigh gets more positive attention and starts to feel that he is not so "medium" after all.
    D. Yes, other students become jealous of his invention and give him an even harder time than before.

4. Why is Leigh glad that he doesn't catch the lunchbox thief?
    A. Catching the thief could have been embarrassing.
    B. He secretly enjoys the daily drama of wondering who the thief is.
    C. He doesn't want to get anyone in trouble because he would have to live with that person for the rest of the school year.
    D. The identity of the thief will always be an unsolved mystery, something fun to think and laugh about for years to come.

5. How does Leigh feel about his burglar alarm invention?
    A. Leigh excited about the invention, but he doesn't like the notoriety it brings him.
    B. Leigh is upset that it didn't work.
    C. Leigh is disappointed in his invention.
    D. Leigh is proud of his invention.

MULTIPLE CHOICE QUESTIONS 11
Dear Mr. Henshaw

Section Eleven: March 16-March 24

1. Why does Leigh keep reading *Ways to Amuse a Dog* over and over again?
    A. His mom says that he should read it.
    B. It reminds him of Bandit.
    C. It is a good book.
    D. Reading it makes him feel good.
2. What concerns does Leigh have about inviting Barry to visit?
    A. Leigh worries that Barry won't like his mom's cooking.
    B. Leigh worries about his house being small and having mildew in the bathroom.
    C. Leigh worries about how Barry will get along with Bandit, that Bandit might not like Barry.
    D. Leigh worries that Barry will not take good care of his books and toys.
3. Which of the following is NOT something Barry likes about visiting Leigh's house?
    A. Barry likes that Leigh has a room no one ever goes into.
    B. Barry likes that he doesn't have to eat with his little sisters at Leigh's house.
    C. Barry likes eating at Leigh's house because the food is good.
    D. Barry likes being able to climb into Leigh's dad's rig when he is visiting.
4. Leigh has a good memory of riding with his dad one day in the truck. What did they do?
    A. They got the truck washed in a special big-rig car wash.
    B. They hauled sugar from the refinery.
    C. They drove all around California.
    D. They hauled grapes to a winery.

MULTIPLE CHOICE QUESTIONS 12
Dear Mr. Henshaw

Section Twelve: March 25-March 31 (end of book)

1. Why does Leigh say he hates his father?
    - A. Leigh's father often does not keep his promises to Leigh. That hurts Leigh, so he says he hates his father.
    - B. Leigh hates that his father is not more like Mr. Henshaw.
    - C. Leigh gets mad because his dad won't take him along on the rig, so he says he hates his father out of anger.
    - D. Leigh says he hates his father to try to make his mother feel better.

2. What does Mrs. Badger like best about "A Day on Dad's Rig"?
    - A. Mrs. Badger likes that "it was written by a boy who wrote honestly about something he knew and had strong feelings about."
    - B. Mrs. Badger likes that his spelling and punctuation are correct and his handwriting is neat.
    - C. Mrs. Badger likes the part about the peak from which Black Bart's lookout used to signal to Black Bart to rob the people coming through the pass.
    - D. Mrs. Badger likes that Leigh wrote about something that was fictional and made completely from his own imagination.

3. Which of the following is NOT a reason why Leigh was often lonely?
    - A. He missed his best friend from his old hometown.
    - B. His Mom worked as a caterer and was not always home in the evening.
    - C. His parents were divorced, so his dad was not at home.
    - D. He didn't have many friends.

4. What does Leigh's story win in the Young Writer's Contest?
    - A. It wins third place.
    - B. It wins second place.
    - C. It wins first place.
    - D. It wins an honorable mention.

5. Who is Angela Badger?
    - A. Angela Badger is Leigh's teacher at school.
    - B. Angela Badger is the real author Leigh gets to have lunch with.
    - C. Angela Badger is the librarian at Leigh's school.
    - D. Angela Badger is a character in one of Mr. Henshaw's books.

6. How does Mrs. Badger describe Mr. Henshaw?
    - A. She describes him as "a sweet older man, slightly gray, with a deeply furrowed brow."
    - B. She describes him as "an amusing and light-hearted fellow, child-like in his attitudes."
    - C. She describes him as "a very nice young man with a wicked twinkle in his eye."
    - D. She describes him as "a grumpy old man."

7. How does Leigh feel when Mrs. Badger calls him an author?
    A. He wishes Mr. Henshaw had called him an author.
    B. He is angry that his parents are not present to hear it.
    C. He is a little embarrassed but very proud.
    D. He wishes his father had called him an author.
8. How does Leigh's dad find Bandit?
    A. One day Leigh's dad discovers Bandit hiding in the back of his rig.
    B. He asks every day over his CB radio and finally gets an answer from a trucker who had picked up a lost dog.
    C. The waitress at the truck stop where Bandit was lost finds Bandit and takes care of him until Leigh's dad returns.
    D. His travels take him back to the stop where he had lost Bandit, and Bandit is still there waiting for him.
9. Why does Leigh give Bandit back to his father?
    A. Leigh thinks his father needs Bandit more than he does.
    B. Leigh thinks having Bandit will make his father more responsible.
    C. Leigh has friends now and doesn't need Bandit.
    D. Leigh gets used to not having Bandit at home.

MULTIPLE CHOICE ANSWER KEY
Dear Mr. Henshaw

	1	2	3	4	5	6	7	8	9	10	11	12
1	C	D	D	B	C	B	D	C	C	D	D	A
2	C	A	D	A	B	D	D	A	A	C	B	A
3	D	C	D		A		D			C	D	A
4	A	B	B				D			C	D	D
5	A	B	D				B			D		B
6	D	D										C
7		A										C
8		D										B
9		D										A

VOCABULARY
Dear Mr. Henshaw Assignment 1

Part I: Using Prior Knowledge and Contextual Clues
Below are the sentences in which the vocabulary words appear in the text. Read the sentence. Use any clues you can find in the sentence combined with your prior knowledge, and write what you think the underlined words mean on the lines provided.

1. The boy's father said city dogs were bored so Joe could not keep the dog unless he could think up seven ways to <u>amuse</u> it. (Page 2)

_____

2. I made a <u>diorama</u> of *Ways to Amuse a Dog*, the book I wrote to you about two times before. (Page 3)

_____

3. Please send me a list of your books that you wrote, an <u>autographed</u> picture and a bookmark. (Page 8)

_____

Part II: Determining the Meaning Match the vocabulary words to their dictionary definitions.

____ 1. amuse   A. having a person's own signature or handwriting

____ 2. diorama   B. a three-dimensional scene in which figures, stuffed wildlife, or other objects are arranged naturalistically against a painted background

____ 3. autographed   C. to occupy in an agreeable, pleasing, or entertaining way

VOCABULARY
Dear Mr. Henshaw Assignment 2

Part I: Using Prior Knowledge and Contextual Clues
Below are the sentences in which the vocabulary words appear in the text. Read the sentence. Use any clues you can find in the sentence combined with your prior knowledge, and write what you think the underlined words mean on the lines provided.

1. Now when the class lines up according to height, I am in the middle. (Page 15)
_____

2. Mom is nagging me about your dumb old questions. (Page 14)
_____

3. Dad used to drive for someone else, hauling stuff like cotton, sugar beets and other produce around Central California and Nevada. (Page 16)

_____

4. Instead of going straight to school, we'd go barreling along the freeway looking down on the tops of ordinary cars, then down the offramp and back to school just before the bell rang. (Page 29)

_____

Part II: Determining the Meaning Match the vocabulary words to their dictionary definitions.

_____ 1. according   A. moving at a high speed

_____ 2. nagging   B. as determined by or in keeping with

_____ 3. hauling   C. scolding, complaining, or constantly finding fault

_____ 4. barreling   D. transporting as with a truck or cart

VOCABULARY
Dear Mr. Henshaw Assignment 3

Part I: Using Prior Knowledge and Contextual Clues

Below are the sentences in which the vocabulary words appear in the text. Read the sentence. Use any clues you can find in the sentence combined with your prior knowledge, and write what you think the underlined words mean on the lines provided.

1. I am sorry I was rude in my last letter when I finished answering your questions. (Page 31)
_____

2. I wish he still hauled sugar beets over to the refinery in Spreckels so he might come to see me. (Page 31)
_____

3. I don't want to be a nuisance to you, but I wish you could tell me how. (Page 36)
_____

Part II: Determining the Meaning Match the vocabulary words to their dictionary definitions.

____ 1. rude   A. an industrial plant for purifying a crude substance such as petroleum or sugar

____ 2. refinery   B. something or someone that is annoying

____ 3. nuisance   C. ill-mannered; discourteous

VOCABULARY
Dear Mr. Henshaw Assignments 4 & 5

Part I: Using Prior Knowledge and Contextual Clues
Below are the sentences in which the vocabulary words appear in the text. Read the sentence. Use any clues you can find in the sentence combined with your prior knowledge, and write what you think the underlined words mean on the lines provided.

1. After Christmas vacation I'll write a <u>fictitious</u> name on my lunchbag. (Page 40)

_____

2. Dad had sent what I always wanted - a <u>quilted</u> down jacket with a lot of pockets and a hood that zips into the collar. (Page 44)

_____

3. Today I wrote a fictitious name, or <u>pseud.</u> as they sometimes say, on my lunchbag. (Page 46)

_____

Part II: Determining the Meaning -- Match the vocabulary words to their dictionary definitions.

____ 1. quilted   A. something that is made up in an author's imagination or is not real

____ 2. fictitious   B. a name used by an author, other than his own; a pen name

____ 3. pseudonym   C. made with layers of fabric stitched together in a pattern

VOCABULARY
Dear Mr. Henshaw Assignment 6

Part I: Using Prior Knowledge and Contextual Clues
Below are the sentences in which the vocabulary words appear in the text. Read the sentence. Use any clues you can find in the sentence combined with your prior knowledge, and write what you think the underlined words mean on the lines provided.

1. At first I was surprised because it wasn't funny like your other books, but then I got to thinking (you said authors should think) and <u>decided</u> a book doesn't have to be funny to be good. (Page 56)

_____

2. When they <u>hibernated</u> and then woke up in the middle of winter because they had eaten all the wrong things and hadn't stored up enough fat, I almost cried. (Page 56)

_____

3. She said our school along with some other schools is going to print (that means <u>mimeograph</u>) a book of work of young authors.... (Page 58)

_____

Part II: Determining the Meaning -- Match the vocabulary words to their dictionary definitions.

____ 1. decided   A. make copies using a stencil and ink using a machine for that purpose

____ 2. hibernated   B. came to a conclusion after thinking about something

____ 3. mimeograph   C. became in an inactive state or period

VOCABULARY
Dear Mr. Henshaw Assignment 7

Part I: Using Prior Knowledge and Contextual Clues

Below are the sentences in which the vocabulary words appear in the text. Read the sentence. Use any clues you can find in the sentence combined with your prior knowledge, and write what you think the underlined words mean on the lines provided.

1. Mr. Fridley noticed me <u>scowling</u> again and said, "So the lunchbag thief strikes again!" (Page 62)

_____

2. I wish I had a grandfather like Mr. Fridley. He is so nice, sort of baggy and <u>comfortable</u>. (Page 62)

_____

3. Sometimes they [truckers] get <u>ulcers</u> from the strain of trying to make good time on the highway. (Page 63)

_____

4. He loves the mountains and the <u>desert</u> sunrises and the sight of orange trees heavy with oranges and the smell of fresh-mown alfalfa. (Page 63)

_____

5. I am filled with <u>wrath</u>. ... I am mad at Mom for divorcing Dad. (Page 64)

_____

6. I was supposed to scrub off some of the <u>mildew</u> on the bathroom walls with some smelly stuff, but I didn't because I was mad at Mom for divorcing Dad. (Page 68)

_____

7. I picked up the <u>receiver</u> and dialed Dad's number over in Bakersfield. (Page 68)

_____

8. "Mountains cut down on <u>reception</u>," Dad told me. (Page 72)

_____

Dear Mr. Henshaw Vocabulary Assignment 7 Page 2

Part II: Determining the Meaning -- Match the vocabulary words to their dictionary definitions.

____ 1. scowling   A. strong anger
____ 2. comfortable B. part of a telephone
____ 3. ulcers   C. at ease; relaxed
____ 4. desert   D. ability to get a transmission or signal
____ 5. wrath   E. a kind of fungus or plant illness caused by fungus
____ 6. mildew   F. having a gloomy or unhappy facial expression
____ 7. receiver   G. very dry region
____ 8. reception   H. skin or other tissue breaking down

VOCABULARY
Dear Mr. Henshaw Assignments 8 & 9

Part I: Using Prior Knowledge and Contextual Clues
Below are the sentences in which the vocabulary words appear in the text. Read the sentence. Use any clues you can find in the sentence combined with your prior knowledge, and write what you think the underlined words mean on the lines provided.

1. I had started down the street past the paint store and <u>antique</u> shops and bakery and all those places and on past the post office when I came to a sign that said BUTTERFLY TREES. (Page 81)

_____

2. Who would want to <u>molest</u> a butterfly? (Page 82)

_____

3. The sticks began to move, and slowly they opened wings and turned into orange and black butterflies, thousands of them <u>quivering</u> on one tree. (Page 82)

_____

4. All the boys in my class are writing <u>weird</u> stories full of monsters, lasers and creatures from outer space. (Page 85)

_____

Part II: Determining the Meaning -- Match the vocabulary words to their dictionary definitions.

_____ 1. antique   A. trembling; shaking

_____ 2. molest   B. strange; bizarre; sometimes involving the supernatural

_____ 3. quivering   C. an old item, sometimes valuable in money or historical significance

_____ 4. weird   D. to bother or interfere with

VOCABULARY
Dear Mr. Henshaw Assignment 10

Part I: Using Prior Knowledge and Contextual Clues
Below are the sentences in which the vocabulary words appear in the text. Read the sentence. Use any clues you can find in the sentence combined with your prior knowledge, and write what you think the underlined words mean on the lines provided.

1. The boys in my class who are writing about monsters just bring in a new monster on the last page to finish off the <u>villains</u> with a laser. (Page 89)

_____

2. Your <u>grateful</u> friend, Leigh (Page 91)

_____

3. While I was looking around for the right kind of <u>insulated</u> wire... (Page 95)

_____

4. Then I went to work <u>fastening</u> one wire from the battery to the switch and from the other side of the switch to the doorbell. (Page 97)

_____

5. I let her in and gave her a <u>demonstration</u> of my burglar alarm. (Page 98)

_____

6. One thing was bothering me. Would my sandwich <u>muffle</u> the bell? (Page 98)

_____

7. The principal, who always <u>prowls</u> around keeping an eye on things at lunchtime, came over to examine my lunchbox. (Page 101)

_____

Dear Mr. Henshaw Vocabulary Assignment 10 Page 2

Part II: Determining the Meaning -- Match the vocabulary words to their dictionary definitions.

____ 1. villains   A. coated; surrounded and isolated

____ 2. grateful   B. walks stealthily, as if hunting

____ 3. insulated   C. thankful

____ 4. fastening   D. a showing of something

____ 5. demonstration   E. evil characters; bad guys

____ 6. muffle   F. attaching

____ 7. prowls   G. make less noisy by covering

VOCABULARY
Dear Mr. Henshaw Assignment 11 & 12

Part I: Using Prior Knowledge and Contextual Clues
Below are the sentences in which the vocabulary words appear in the text. Read the sentence. Use any clues you can find in the sentence combined with your prior knowledge, and write what you think the underlined words mean on the lines provided.

1. I really didn't know what to say to my father. It was embarrassing. (Page 105)

_____

2. He's a good driver, but he speeds to make time whenever he can avoid the highway patrol. (Page 107)

_____

3. I thought I might write about them [the butterflies] in prose instead of poetry... (Page 107)

_____

4. Mom cooked a casserole full of good things like ground beef, chilies, tortillas, tomatoes and cheese. (Page 110)

_____

5. I have noticed that authors like Mr. Henshaw usually wear old plaid shirts in the pictures on the back of their books. (Page 115)

_____

6. *A Day on Dad's Rig* was splendid work for a boy your age. (Page 119)

_____

7. You wrote like *you*, and you did not try to imitate someone else. (Page 119)

_____

Dear Mr. Henshaw Vocabulary Assignment 11-12 Page 2

Part II: Determining the Meaning -- Match the vocabulary words to their dictionary definitions.

____ 1. embarrassing   A. Ordinary sentences; without poetic form

____ 2. avoid   B. To act or do as another has acted or done

____ 3. prose   C. A pattern of horizontal and vertical lines of different colors

____ 4. casserole   D. Try to keep away from

____ 5. plaid   E. Wonderful; excellent; great

____ 6. splendid   F. Making a person feel ashamed or uncomfortable

____ 7. imitate   G. Mixture of foods baked in a single dish

VOCABULARY ANSWER KEY
Dear Mr. Henshaw

	1	2	3	4 & 5	6	7	8 & 9	10	11&12
1	C	B	C	C	B	F	C	E	F
2	B	C	A	A	C	C	D	C	D
3	A	D	B	B	A	H	A	A	A
4		A				G	B	F	G
5						A		D	C
6						E		G	E
7						B		B	B
8						D			

QUOTATIONS
Dear Mr. Henshaw

Here are some important quotations from Dear Mr. Henshaw. You could use these in a variety of ways:
- Assign one to each student or a few to groups of students
- Put them on a bulletin board for class discussion
- Write each one on a piece of paper and play the crumpled paper/trash can game with them. (Crumple them up, put them in a clean trash can, let each student pick one out and explain the significance of the quote, then let students shoot baskets with the paper wads to return them to the can for another round...or for another class.)

1. Dear Mr. Henshaw, I am the boy who wrote to you last year when I was in the second grade. (December 3)
2. I guess you could call me the mediumest boy in the class. (November 20)
3. The kids here pay more attention to my lunch than they do to me. (November 27)
4. Well, keep your nose clean, kid. (December 1)
5. Mom said one shoe sounded sad, like a country-western song. (December 24)
6. It was a lovely dinner for lonely hearts. (December 25)
7. I guess I'm really afraid I might find another man who's in love with a truck. (January 10)
8. Now I know Mr. Fridley isn't the only one who notices me. (January 12)
9. I wonder what happens to the fathers of bears. (January 15)
10. I don't think Dad is that much interested in me. He didn't phone when he said he would. (January 15)
11. Don't think you are the only boy around here with a father who forgets. (January 20)
12. If Dad loves all those things so much, why can't he love me? (January 30)
13. Bandit and I didn't get a divorce. They did. (January 31)
14. Most truckers ate real fast and left, but Dad kidded around for a while and played the video games. (February 2)
15. "Take it easy, kid," he said. "I just didn't get around to it. I was going to call this evening. The week isn't over yet." (February 4)
16. There was a funny silence. For a minute I thought the line was dead. Then I knew something must have happened to my dog. (February 4)
17. Hey, Bill, Mom wants to know when we're going out to get the pizza? (February 4)
18. I can't hate him. Maybe things would be easier if I could. (February 5)
19. I enjoyed riding with him until you came along, and--well, by that time I had had enough of highways and truck stops. (February 5)
20. ...whenever I watch the waves, I always feel that no matter how bad things seem, life will still go on. (February 5)

Dear Mr. Henshaw Quotations Page 2

21. The California bear was right side up so maybe Mr. Fridley didn't need me to help him after all. (February 6)
22. Maybe you don't [care], but I do. (February 6)
23. Sorry about Bandit. Here's $20. Go buy yourself an ice cream cone. (February 9)
24. The man is made of wax, and every time he crosses the desert, he melts a little. (February 15)
25. Sometimes I start a letter to Dad thanking him for the twenty dollars, but I can't finish that either. I don't know why. (March 2)
26. What are you planning to make, son? (March 3)
27. I began to feel like some sort of hero. Maybe I'm not so medium after all. (March 5)
28. I don't like to think about Dad being lonesome, but I don't like to think about the pizza boy cheering him up, either. (March 25)
29. "Your father isn't a bad man by any means." (March 25)
30. Some kids were mad because they didn't win or even get something printed. They said they wouldn't ever try to write again which I think is pretty dumb. I have heard that real authors sometimes have their books turned down. I figure you win some, you lose some. (March 26)
31. She called me an author. *A real live author called me an author.* (March 30)
32. I didn't think answers to those questions were very important. (March 30)
33. Dad's stomach hung over his belt, and he wasn't as tall as I remembered him. (March 31)
34. After all these months when I had longed to see him, it took a load of broccoli to get him here. I felt let down and my feelings hurt. He rumpled my hair and said, "You're smarter than your old man." That embarrassed me. I didn't know how to answer. (March 31)
35. "So long, son," he said. "I'll try to get over to see you more often."
    "Sure, Dad," I said. I had learned by now that I couldn't count on anything he said. (March 31)
36. Dad, you keep Bandit. You need him more than I do. ... Please take him. I don't have any way to amuse him. (March 31)

BULLETIN BOARD IDEAS
Dear Mr. Henshaw

1. Save a space for **students' best writing**. Make a border or graphic that illustrates the topic of their writing. Staple up the best writing samples (or quizzes or whatever you have graded) on colorful paper.

2. Students should be encouraged to talk about **other books by Beverly Cleary** that they have read and also encouraged to read other Beverly Cleary books for their self-selected reading.

A bulletin board could be made of book covers from books students have read or read during the unit. Each book cover should be significant to the book it represents. Use the cover of *Dear Mr. Henshaw* as an example of a cover that is significant to the story.

This will help students to find main events in a story and also to read self-selected books beyond the books read in class. Beverly Cleary is so popular with students that reading her books may get some students more interested in reading on their own.

3. Draw one of the **word search puzzles** onto the bulletin board. (Be sure to enlarge it.) Write the key words to one side. Invite students to take their pens or markers and find the words before and/or after class (or perhaps this could be an activity for students who finish their work early).

4. Place a **map of the United States** on the board and mark the various places mentioned in the book.

5. Have students bring in **pictures of single shoes** of all different types. Post students' "shoe songs" among the shoes.

6. Post pictures of lots of different **good things to eat, like were stolen from Leigh's lunches**. Label each and include a little stack of recipes (on 1/4 sheets of paper, stapled or pinned in a stack) next to each picture so students can take the recipes of the things that look good to them and try to make it! If they make the things, have them write comments or ratings on the board.

7. Make a bulletin board about **adopting a dog**, how to care for a dog...perhaps even Ways To Amuse A Dog! Use pictures of dogs from your local humane society (usually posted on line).

8. Get pictures of **different kinds of trucks**—grain trucks, oil trucks, refrigerated trucks, delivery trucks, etc. and post them on the board with information about how to become a truck driver, careers in the trucking industry, etc.

EXTRA ACTIVITIES
Dear Mr. Henshaw

One of the difficulties in teaching a novel is that all students don't read at the same speed. One student who likes to read may take the book home and finish it in a day or two. Sometimes a few students finish the in-class assignments early. The problem, then, is finding suitable extra activities for students.

One thing you can do is keep a little library in the classroom. For this unit on *Dear Mr. Henshaw*, you might check out from the school library other books by Beverly Cleary. A biography of the author would be interesting for some students. You may include other related books and articles about: trucking, divorce, catering, becoming a writer, writing, dog care, electricity, how to make an alarm, famous authors, cleaning mildew (and other things), being a single parent, conflict resolution, your school's literary magazine or yearbook, etc.

Other things you may keep on hand are puzzles. We have made some relating directly to *Dear Mr. Henshaw* for you. Feel free to duplicate them for your students.

1. Pick a chapter or scene with a great deal of dialogue and have the students act it out on a stage. (Perhaps you could assign various scenes to different groups of students so more than one scene could be acted and more students could participate

2. Create a Cereal Box Book for *Dear Mr. Henshaw*. Students take an empty cereal box, cover it with construction paper and turn it into what looks like a large book. *Front panel*: title, illustration, author, and short summary. *First side*: List of characters *Second side or spine*: Name of book (*Dear Mr. Henshaw*) *Back panel*: Game or contest pertaining to book These look nice lined up next to each other like a real shelf of books. (Encourage a variety of paper colors, inks, markers, etc.)

3. Promote model builders to try to make a lunch box alarm like Leigh's.

4. Invite a guest speaker: an author, a truck driver, a caterer, a person from the humane society, or a counselor (to discuss conflict resolution).

5. Have a "hero" day during which students can each tell about a person they idolize or admire.

6. Have students plan and teach a lesson on a chapter or section of the book. Give them guidelines and a time-frame.

7. Have students each write a letter to their favorite authors (preferably living).

8. Write a diary entry for the day grown-up Leigh finally meets Mr. Henshaw, years later.

RELATED TOPICS
Dear Mr. Henshaw

Here are some topics related to *Dear Mr. Henshaw*. They could be used as research or nonfiction reading topics, as topics for guest speakers, or in any other way you might create.

Letter writing
Famous authors
Other Beverly Cleary books
Transportation
Kinds of trucks
Hibernation
Divorce
Families
Catering
Alarms and alarm systems
State flags
Refineries
Moose
Having a dog as a pet
Careers in trucking, nursing, writing, teaching, or owning a store
Ways to amuse a dog
Loneliness
Fitting in at a new school
Responsibility
Parenting

UNIT WORD LIST
Dear Mr. Henshaw

1. ALARM — Mr. Fridley gave Leigh the idea for this.
2. ALASKA — Mr. Henshaw moves to this state that has moose.
3. BADGER — She is the Famous Author the kids met for lunch.
4. BANDIT — Leigh's dog
5. BARRY — Friend from school who eats dinner with Leigh
6. BOTTS — Last name of Leigh, Bonnie, and Bill
7. BUTTERFLY — Leigh visits the ___ trees.
8. CALIFORNIA — State where Leigh and his mom live
9. CANAPES — Special little food items for Leigh's lunch
10. CLEARY — Author of *Dear Mr. Henshaw*
11. DIARY — Special book Leigh writes in
12. FRIDLEY — He asks Leigh to help with the flag at school.
13. GARBAGE — Mr. Fridley sometimes guards this.
14. HENSHAW — Author of *Ways to Amuse a Dog*
15. JACKET — Christmas present from Dad
16. JOE — Fictitious name on Leigh's lunch
17. KATY — Bonnie's catering boss
18. LEIGH — He is the protagonist, the main character in the story.
19. LIBRARIAN — She saved Mr. Henshaw's new book for Leigh.
20. MARTINEZ — Leigh's teacher
21. MONSTERS — Most of the boys wrote about these.
22. PIZZA — I wonder if Dad will marry the ___ boy and his mother.
23. PROMISES — Dad doesn't keep his ___ to Leigh.
24. QUESTIONS — Having to answer these made Leigh mad at first.
25. RAIN — It signals a low point or troubling time in the story.
26. RIG — Nickname for Leigh's dad's truck
27. SHOES — Mom, Dad, and Leigh made up silly songs about these.
28. SPRECKELS — The refinery there shut down.
29. WAX — Leigh first writes about a ten-foot ___ man.
30. WRITER — Leigh wants to be this when he grows up.
31. YELLOWSTONE — Setting for *Beggar Bears*

WORD SEARCH
Dear Mr. Henshaw

Y	K	H	C	A	L	I	F	O	R	N	I	A	Z	C	B
E	R	H	A	J	S	T	B	X	G	P	J	X	C	L	U
L	K	G	N	B	K	X	A	S	J	I	R	F	F	E	T
L	R	G	A	Q	D	F	D	P	C	Z	L	N	R	A	T
O	A	K	P	R	V	S	G	R	Q	Z	V	Y	I	R	E
W	L	K	E	K	B	B	E	E	J	A	K	N	D	Y	R
S	A	Y	S	A	J	A	R	C	W	A	D	Q	L	B	F
T	R	H	X	T	J	Z	G	K	R	L	C	C	E	R	L
O	M	S	E	Y	R	O	L	E	I	G	H	K	Y	Y	Y
N	W	M	G	N	G	Z	E	L	T	V	Y	X	E	F	Q
E	M	L	O	D	S	G	V	S	E	F	W	B	W	T	C
B	C	P	X	N	X	H	B	Z	R	B	S	P	V	F	T
O	S	H	O	E	S	R	A	I	N	A	L	A	S	K	A
T	V	S	R	F	L	T	P	W	R	N	G	T	T	M	C
T	P	R	O	M	I	S	E	S	I	D	W	T	V	C	H
S	D	I	A	R	Y	B	T	R	G	I	B	A	R	R	Y
Q	U	E	S	T	I	O	N	S	S	T	C	H	X	G	W

Author of *Dear Mr. Henshaw* (6)
Author of *Ways to Amuse a Dog* (7)
Bonnie's catering boss (4)
Christmas present from Dad (6)
Dad doesn't keep his ___ to Leigh. (8)
Fictitious name on Leigh's lunch (3)
Friend from school who eats dinner with Leigh (5)
Having to answer these made Leigh mad at first. (9)
He asks Leigh to help with the flag at school. (7)
He is the protagonist, the main character in the story. (5)
I wonder if Dad will marry the ___ boy and his mother. (5)
It signals a low point or troubling time in the story. (4)
Last name of Leigh, Bonnie, and Bill (5)
Leigh first writes about a ten-foot ___ man. (3)
Leigh visits the ___ trees. (9)
Leigh wants to be this when he grows up. (6)
Leigh's dog (6)
Mom, Dad, and Leigh made up silly songs about these. (5)
Most of the boys wrote about these. (8)
Mr. Fridley gave Leigh the idea for this. (5)
Mr. Fridley sometimes guards this. (7)
Mr. Henshaw moves to this state that has moose. (6)
Nickname for Leigh's dad's truck (3)
Setting for Beggar Bears (11)
She is the Famous Author the kids met for lunch. (6)
Special book Leigh writes in (5)
Special little food items for Leigh's lunch (7)
State where Leigh and his mom live (10)
The refinery there shut down. (9)

WORD SEARCH ANSWER KEY
Dear Mr. Henshaw

```
Y           C   A   L   I   F   O   R   N   I   A           C   B
E           A           B           P                       L   U
L       G   N           A   S       I               F       E   T
L           A           D   P       Z               R       A   T
O   A       P   R       G   R       Z               I       R   E
W   L       E   K   B   G   E   J   A               D       Y   R
S   A       S   A       A   R   C   W   A           L           F
T   R   H       T   J       G   K   R       C       E           L
O   M       E   Y       O   L   E   I   G   H   K   Y           Y
N       M       N           E   L   T               E
E           O       S           S   E                   T
B               N       H       R   B
O   S   H   O   E   S   R   A   I   N   A   L   A   S   K   A
T                       T       W   R   N
T   P   R   O   M   I   S   E   S   I   D   W
S   D   I   A   R   Y           R   G   I   B   A   R   R   Y
Q   U   E   S   T   I   O   N   S   S   T           X
```

Author of *Dear Mr. Henshaw* (6)
Author of *Ways to Amuse a Dog* (7)
Bonnie's catering boss (4)
Christmas present from Dad (6)
Dad doesn't keep his ___ to Leigh. (8)
Fictitious name on Leigh's lunch (3)
Friend from school who eats dinner with Leigh (5)
Having to answer these made Leigh mad at first. (9)
He asks Leigh to help with the flag at school. (7)
He is the protagonist, the main character in the story. (5)
I wonder if Dad will marry the ___ boy and his mother. (5)
It signals a low point or troubling time in the story. (4)
Last name of Leigh, Bonnie, and Bill (5)
Leigh first writes about a ten-foot ___ man. (3)
Leigh visits the ___ trees. (9)
Leigh wants to be this when he grows up. (6)
Leigh's dog (6)
Mom, Dad, and Leigh made up silly songs about these. (5)
Most of the boys wrote about these. (8)
Mr. Fridley gave Leigh the idea for this. (5)
Mr. Fridley sometimes guards this. (7)
Mr. Henshaw moves to this state that has moose. (6)
Nickname for Leigh's dad's truck (3)
Setting for Beggar Bears (11)
She is the Famous Author the kids met for lunch. (6)
Special book Leigh writes in (5)
Special little food items for Leigh's lunch (7)
State where Leigh and his mom live (10)
The refinery there shut down. (9)

CROSSWORD
Dear Mr. Henshaw

Across
1. State where Leigh and his mom live
4. I wonder if Dad will marry the ___ boy and his mother.
6. Leigh first writes about a ten-foot ___ man.
7. She is the Famous Author the kids met for lunch.
9. Fictitious name on Leigh's lunch
10. It signals a low point or troubling time in the story.
11. Bonnie's catering boss
12. Leigh wants to be this when he grows up.
13. Leigh visits the ___ trees.

Down
1. Special little food items for Leigh's lunch
2. He asks Leigh to help with the flag at school.
3. Mr. Henshaw moves to this state that has moose.
4. Dad doesn't keep his ___ to Leigh.
5. He is the protagonist, the main character in the story.
7. Friend from school who eats dinner with Leigh
8. Most of the boys wrote about these.
9. Christmas present from Dad
10. Nickname for Leigh's dad's truck

CROSSWORD ANSWER KEY
Dear Mr. Henshaw

				1				2				3		
				C	A	L	I	F	O	R	N	I	A	
4														
P	I	Z	Z	A				R				L		
										5		6		
R				N				I		L		W	A	X
						7								8
O				A		B	A	D	G	E	R		S	M
M				P		A		L		I			K	O
		9										10		
I		J	O	E		R		E		G		R	A	I	N
S		A		S		R		Y		H		I		S
E		C				Y						G		T
		11												
S		K	A	T	Y									E
											12			
		E								W	R	I	T	E	R
13														
B	U	T	T	E	R	F	L	Y						S

Across
1. State where Leigh and his mom live
4. I wonder if Dad will marry the ___ boy and his mother.
6. Leigh first writes about a ten-foot ___ man.
7. She is the Famous Author the kids met for lunch.
9. Fictitious name on Leigh's lunch
10. It signals a low point or troubling time in the story.
11. Bonnie's catering boss
12. Leigh wants to be this when he grows up.
13. Leigh visits the ___ trees.

Down
1. Special little food items for Leigh's lunch
2. He asks Leigh to help with the flag at school.
3. Mr. Henshaw moves to this state that has moose.
4. Dad doesn't keep his ___ to Leigh.
5. He is the protagonist, the main character in the story.
7. Friend from school who eats dinner with Leigh
8. Most of the boys wrote about these.
9. Christmas present from Dad
10. Nickname for Leigh's dad's truck

VOCABULARY WORD LIST
Dear Mr. Henshaw

1. ACCORDING — As determined by or in keeping with
2. AMUSE — To occupy in an agreeable, pleasing, or entertaining way
3. ANTIQUE — An old item, sometimes valuable
4. AUTOGRAPHED — Having a person's own signature or handwriting
5. BARRELING — Moving at high speed
6. COMFORTABLE — At ease; relaxed
7. DECIDED — Came to a conclusion after thinking about something
8. DEMONSTRATION — A showing of something, like a process or how something works
9. DESERT — Very dry region
10. DIORAMA — 3-D scene with objects against a painted background
11. FASTENING — Attaching
12. FICTITIOUS — Made-up; not real
13. GRATEFUL — Thankful
14. HAULING — Transporting as with a truck or cart
15. HIBERNATED — Became in an inactive state for a period of time
16. INSULATED — Coated; surrounded and isolated
17. MILDEW — A kind of fungus
18. MIMEOGRAPH — Make copies using a stencil and ink, using a machine for that purpose
19. MOLEST — To bother or interfere with
20. MUFFLE — Make less noisy by covering
21. NAGGING — Scolding, complaining, or constantly finding fault
22. NUISANCE — Something or someone that is annoying
23. PROWLS — Walks stealthily, as if hunting
24. PSEUDONYM — A pen-name
25. QUILTED — Made with layers of fabric stitched together in a pattern
26. QUIVERING — Trembling; shaking
27. RECEIVER — Part of a telephone
28. RECEPTION — Ability to get a transmission or signal
29. REFINERY — An industrial plant for purifying a crude substance such as oil or sugar
30. RUDE — Having bad manners
31. SCOWLING — Having a gloomy or unhappy facial expression
32. ULCERS — Skin or other tissue break-down
33. VILLAINS — Evil characters; bad guys
34. WEIRD — Strange; bizarre; sometimes involving the supernatural
35. WRATH — Strong anger

VOCABULARY WORD SEARCH
Dear Mr. Henshaw

P	R	O	W	L	S	W	N	H	D	I	O	R	A	M	A
J	B	N	Q	H	P	E	V	I	L	L	A	I	N	S	T
M	D	A	U	A	N	I	G	B	S	K	L	N	V	Z	K
I	G	G	I	U	M	R	B	E	X	G	X	Q	S	L	X
M	F	G	V	L	S	D	A	R	C	R	D	N	T	W	Z
E	N	I	E	I	D	L	M	N	E	K	E	C	L	C	Z
O	D	N	R	N	C	E	U	A	D	F	C	L	S	O	Y
G	P	G	I	G	F	A	S	T	E	N	I	N	G	M	R
R	R	S	N	Y	V	W	E	E	Q	W	D	N	G	F	B
A	J	A	G	K	Q	T	S	D	R	N	E	R	E	O	C
P	Y	D	T	Y	H	U	X	H	W	T	D	E	U	R	N
H	R	E	C	E	P	T	I	O	N	M	L	C	L	T	Y
V	W	M	U	F	F	L	E	L	N	O	D	E	C	A	K
M	I	L	D	E	W	U	R	P	T	L	J	I	E	B	W
A	N	T	I	Q	U	E	L	B	G	E	Z	V	R	L	R
N	U	I	S	A	N	C	E	R	N	S	D	E	S	E	C
W	R	A	T	H	R	U	D	E	F	T	F	R	N	Z	C

3-D scene with objects against a painted background (7)

A kind of fungus (6)

Ability to get a transmission or signal (9)

An industrial plant for purifying a crude substance such as oil or sugar (8)

An old item, sometimes valuable (7)

At ease; relaxed (11)

Attaching (9)

Became in an inactive state for a period of time (10)

Came to a conclusion after thinking about something (7)

Evil characters; bad guys (8)

Having bad manners (4)

Made with layers of fabric stitched together in a pattern (7)

Make copies using a stencil and ink, using a machine for that purpose (10)

Make less noisy by covering (6)

Part of a telephone (8)

Scolding, complaining, or constantly finding fault (7)

Skin or other tissue break-down (6)

Something or someone that is annoying (8)

Strange; bizarre; sometimes involving the supernatural (5)

Strong anger (5)

Thankful (8)

To bother or interfere with (6)

To occupy in an agreeable, pleasing, or entertaining way (5)

Transporting as with a truck or cart (7)

Trembling; shaking (9)

Very dry region (6)

Walks stealthily, as if hunting (6)

VOCABULARY WORD SEARCH ANSWER KEY
Dear Mr. Henshaw

```
P   R   O   W   L   S   W       H   D   I   O   R   A   M   A
    N   Q   H       E   V   I   L   L   A   I   N   S
M   A   U   A       I       B
I   G   I   U       R       E
M   G   V   L       D   A   R       D
E   I   E   I   D       M   N   E   E               C
O   N   R   N       E   U   A   F   C               O
G   G   I   G   F   A   S   T   E   N   I   N   G   M
R   R       N           E   E       D   N           F
A   A       G       Q       D   R       E   R   E   O
P       T           U           T   D   E   U       R
H   R   E   C   E   P   T   I   O   N   M       C   L   T   Y
        M   U   F   F   L   E   L       O       E   C   A
M   I   L   D   E   W   U           T   L       I   E   B
A   N   T   I   Q   U   E   L               E   V   R   L
N   U   I   S   A   N   C   E               S   D   E   S   E
W   R   A   T   H   R   U   D   E           T       R
```

3-D scene with objects against a painted background (7)

A kind of fungus (6)

Ability to get a transmission or signal (9)

An industrial plant for purifying a crude substance such as oil or sugar (8)

An old item, sometimes valuable (7)

At ease; relaxed (11)

Attaching (9)

Became in an inactive state for a period of time (10)

Came to a conclusion after thinking about something (7)

Evil characters; bad guys (8)

Having bad manners (4)

Made with layers of fabric stitched together in a pattern (7)

Make copies using a stencil and ink, using a machine for that purpose (10)

Make less noisy by covering (6)

Part of a telephone (8)

Scolding, complaining, or constantly finding fault (7)

Skin or other tissue break-down (6)

Something or someone that is annoying (8)

Strange; bizarre; sometimes involving the supernatural (5)

Strong anger (5)

Thankful (8)

To bother or interfere with (6)

To occupy in an agreeable, pleasing, or entertaining way (5)

Transporting as with a truck or cart (7)

Trembling; shaking (9)

Very dry region (6)

Walks stealthily, as if hunting (6)

VOCABULARY WORD SEARCH 2
Dear Mr. Henshaw

```
R  U  D  E  P  R  O  W  L  S  G  R  A  A  N  P
N  W  V  P  M  D  D  R  R  Z  R  M  M  C  U  Y
P  W  V  H  I  E  I  E  W  A  A  S  U  C  I  V
C  F  R  R  L  M  O  C  E  M  T  Q  S  O  S  D
Z  O  Y  K  D  O  R  E  I  P  E  H  E  R  A  C
L  D  M  G  E  N  A  I  R  Q  F  Q  Y  D  N  Q
M  S  F  F  W  S  M  V  D  H  U  P  L  I  C  Z
G  M  M  B  O  T  A  E  D  S  L  I  Y  N  E  J
N  D  E  S  E  R  T  R  W  F  R  Y  L  G  P  V
I  N  S  U  L  A  T  E  D  H  F  G  K  T  S  C
R  W  J  D  Y  T  P  A  N  D  A  Z  Y  A  E  J
T  E  J  E  Q  I  T  G  B  F  S  U  W  N  U  D
M  Y  F  C  W  O  D  Y  H  L  T  B  L  T  D  X
X  O  N  I  J  N  S  U  L  C  E  R  S  I  O  W
W  M  L  D  N  N  A  G  G  I  N  G  H  Q  N  Q
B  D  D  E  R  E  C  E  P  T  I  O  N  U  Y  G
Y  S  V  D  S  K  R  X  J  X  N  C  F  E  M  F
K  T  D  W  V  T  L  Y  Y  V  G  T  Y  J  Z  T
```

ACCORDING	MOLEST
AMUSE	NAGGING
ANTIQUE	NUISANCE
COMFORTABLE	PROWLS
DECIDED	PSEUDONYM
DEMONSTRATION	QUILTED
DESERT	RECEIVER
DIORAMA	RECEPTION
FASTENING	REFINERY
GRATEFUL	RUDE
HAULING	ULCERS
INSULATED	WEIRD
MILDEW	WRATH

VOCABULARY WORD SEARCH 2 ANSWER KEY
Dear Mr. Henshaw

```
R  U  D  E     P  R  O  W  L  S     G        A     A  N
               M  D  D  R     R     R        M     C  U
               I  E  I  E  W  A     A        U     C  I
C              L  M  O  C  E  T     E        S  H  E  R  A
   O           D  O  R  E  I  E     H        E     D  N
      M        E  N  A  I  R  Q     F           D  I  N
         F  W  S  M  V  D     U                 N  N  C
               O  T  A  E     L              I     G  E
   D  E  S  E  R  T  R                          L  G  P
I  N  S  U  L  A  T  E  D     H     F              T  S
R        D     T     A              A              A  E
   E     E     I           B           S  U        N     D
M     F  C     O                 L        T     L  T  U
   O     I     N     U  L  C  E  R  S     I     D  O
      L  D     N  A  G  G  I  N  G              Q  N
            E  R  E  C  E  P  T  I  O     N     U  Y  G
               D  S     R                 N        E  M
                  T        Y              G
```

ACCORDING	MOLEST
AMUSE	NAGGING
ANTIQUE	NUISANCE
COMFORTABLE	PROWLS
DECIDED	PSEUDONYM
DEMONSTRATION	QUILTED
DESERT	RECEIVER
DIORAMA	RECEPTION
FASTENING	REFINERY
GRATEFUL	RUDE
HAULING	ULCERS
INSULATED	WEIRD
MILDEW	WRATH

VOCABULARY CROSSWORD
Dear Mr. Henshaw

Across
1. An old item, sometimes valuable
5. Having bad manners
6. Coated; surrounded and isolated
8. Came to a conclusion after thinking about something
10. Scolding, complaining, or constantly finding fault
11. Walks stealthily, as if hunting
12. As determined by or in keeping with
13. Became in an inactive state for a period of time

Down
1. To occupy in an agreeable, pleasing, or entertaining way
2. Trembling; shaking
3. Make less noisy by covering
4. Very dry region
7. Having a person's own signature or handwriting
8. 3-D scene with objects against a painted background
9. Moving at high speed

VOCABULARY CROSSWORD ANSWER KEY
Dear Mr. Henshaw

	1 A	N	T	I	2 Q	U	E						
	M				U			3 M			4 D		
5 R	U	D	E		6 I	N	S	U	L	7 A	T	E	D
	S				V			F		U		S	
8 D	E	C	I	D	E	D		F		T		E		9 B
I					R			L		O		R		A
O					I			E		G		T		R
R					N			R		R				R
A		10 N	A	G	G	I	N	G		A				E
M								11 P	R	O	W	L	S
12 A	C	C	O	R	D	I	N	G		H				I
								E						N
	13 H	I	B	E	R	N	A	T	E	D				G

Across
1. An old item, sometimes valuable
5. Having bad manners
6. Coated; surrounded and isolated
8. Came to a conclusion after thinking about something
10. Scolding, complaining, or constantly finding fault
11. Walks stealthily, as if hunting
12. As determined by or in keeping with
13. Became in an inactive state for a period of time

Down
1. To occupy in an agreeable, pleasing, or entertaining way
2. Trembling; shaking
3. Make less noisy by covering
4. Very dry region
7. Having a person's own signature or handwriting
8. 3-D scene with objects against a painted background
9. Moving at high speed

www.ingramcontent.com/pod-product-compliance
Lightning Source LLC
Chambersburg PA
CBHW051403070526
44584CB00023B/3278